THE FACTS ABOUT
CHILD SEXUAL ABUSE

TITLES IN THE FACTS ABOUT ... SERIES

THE FACTS ABOUT
CHILD SEXUAL ABUSE

BILL GILLHAM

CASSELL

Cassell Educational Limited
Villiers House
41/47 Strand
London WC2N 5JE

First published 1991

British Library Cataloguing in Publication Data
Gillham, W. E. C. (William Edwin Charles) *1936–*
    The facts about child sexual abuse. – (The Facts About . . .
    series)
    1. Children. Sexual abuse by adults
    I. Title
    362.76

ISBN 0–304–32262–8 (hardback)
    0–304–32272–5 (paperback)

Typeset by Fakenham Photosetting Limited, Fakenham, Norfolk
Printed and bound in Great Britain by Biddles Ltd, Guildford and King's Lynn

CONTENTS

Contents

SERIES FOREWORD

The idea for this series came from an awareness that much of the media hype, and some of the professional practice, relating to major social problems involving children and adolescents was singularly ill-informed. At the same time there was a notable lack of short, accessible summaries of the relevant research data by which people could inform themselves.

Not surprisingly, the conclusions that are drawn from a careful consideration of the evidence challenge many generally held assumptions – at all levels of popular and professional concern.

Bill Gillham

ACKNOWLEDGEMENTS

Acknowledgement is gratefully given to Judith Gillham for editorial assistance in the detailed preparation of the manuscript and to Chris Bailey of Strathclyde University's Andersonian Library for expert advice and help in carrying out on-line searches. The following authors and publishers have kindly given permission to reproduce copyright figures and tables: J. Jason, S. L. Williams, A. Burton and R. Rochat and The American Medical Association for Figure 2.1; L. E. Budin and C. F. Johnson and Pergamon Press for Figure 6.1; N. J. Wild and The British Medical Association for Table 2.1; G. F. Indest and Brunner-Mazel Inc. for Table 4.1; F. Sink and The American Orthopsychiatric Association Inc. for Table 4.2; R. J. Goldman and J. D. G. Goldman and The Family Life Movement of Australia for Table 5.1; C. L. Nash and D. J. West and the Gower Publishing Company for Table 5.3; J. T. Landis and Human Sciences Press Inc. for Tables 2.5 and 5.2.

1

DEFINING THE PROBLEM

INTRODUCTION

One of the surprising things about child sexual abuse is its recency as a topic of general concern. Even in the professional and academic literature there are few references before the late 1970s and almost none before the beginning of that decade. It is worth noting, however, that two of the most substantial empirical studies, by Landis (1956) and Gagnon (1965), are to be found in this earlier period, apparently attracting little attention at the time.

Why was the topic so neglected? It is difficult to be sure but the likely answer is the simple one: that to most people the sexual abuse of children was unthinkable, intuitively incredible except in the case of a small number of seriously disturbed individuals. If you do not believe that such behaviour is widespread then you will tend not to notice any evidence, or to interpret the evidence differently. Child sexual abuse is, in any case, a secret activity, something that those involved usually do not reveal, whether victim or perpetrator.

All sexual behaviour is relatively secret. Despite the fact that sex is now more talked about, in a general way, than it was twenty or thirty years ago, on the whole people do *not* disclose their sexual behaviour. For example, of the people we know well – friends and colleagues, say – how much do we actually know about their sexual behaviour? There is a parallel gap in empirical research. At this level we have remarkably little knowledge about human behaviour. The most comprehensive investigations to date, with all their methodological flaws (the recruitment of subjects was idiosyncratic to say the least), are the Kinsey Reports of the late 1940s and early 1950s (Kinsey *et al.*, 1948, 1953). The study by Gagnon cited above is a further analysis of a subsample of the female subjects in the Kinsey study.

Much has been made of the fact that Freud, having initially accepted as true the reports of incest by his female patients, finally came to regard them as fantasies. Masson's book (Masson, 1984) deals with this subject at length, but Gagnon sums it up as follows:

> Freud was at first convinced that his patients were reporting actual events when they told him of their childhood sexual experiences with adults, especially parents. He thought this intervention by an adult in the sexual development of the child to be a necessary element in the formation of adult hysterias. This insight represented an original breakthrough from which Freud generalized that the roots of all adult neuroses lay in childhood sexual contacts with adults or in extensive contacts with peers. Freud reversed this view first in one of his letters to Fleiss and later in print in 'My Views on the Part Played by Sexuality in the Aetiology of the Neuroses' (1905). The reports of childhood seductions now appeared to be defenses against the actual sexual behavior (usually masturbation) of the child. In a major sense this conversion of the patients' reports from actual events into universal fantasies served to broaden and extend the scope of the theory and to give it greater generality since the adult disorder no longer depended upon the presence or absence of a specific seduction. From the specific instance of an adult seduction of a child Freud was led to the larger formulation of the Oedipus Complex. (p. 177)

There is nothing in Freud's history to suggest that he was prone to suppressing uncomfortable truths, and it would seem even more unreasonable to claim that he determined the course of subsequent events in the concealment of the problem. At the point when he made that interpretive change his work was relatively little known. It was not until the 1920s that Freud became widely influential, and by that time the earlier theoretical shift was well buried. Freud discounted what he was told because he felt that it was incredible and in that respect he was no different from his contemporaries, or many people to this day. Of more significance is the fact that if Freud was wrong (and we can't *know* that he was wrong about those particular patients) then much of his subsequent theoretical edifice falls to the ground. Note that another related assumption – the supposed 'sexual latency' period between infancy and puberty – is also overturned by recent empirical research (Goldman and Goldman, 1988).

But that is history and it cannot be rewritten. Our priorities now are to gain a balanced perspective. One of the problems with the current level of concern is the amount of professional activity which is misdirected, based on inadequate evidence or a prejudiced interpretation.

The strident indignation of some writers (e.g. Driver, 1989) often seems to imply that abuse is part of the sexual orientation of all men. The realm of sexual politics is only one source of evidence interpretation and distortion; professional rivalry is another; the 'bandwagon' effect is yet another. It is because of these unbalancing forces that the present book focuses on empirical research findings. If society is to take effective action then that action must be based on the most accurate knowledge we have, and on a reasonable interpretation of it.

WHAT IS MEANT BY CHILD SEXUAL ABUSE?

There is no shortage of definitions. Fraser (1981) proposes: 'the exploitation of a child for the sexual gratification of an adult' (p. 58). Few would quarrel with this, but it is not nearly precise enough. To begin with: what is a child? (And, by implication, what is an adult?) Even a simple definition in terms of the legal age of consent is not straightforward, as this refers to the age valid in law at which a *girl* can consent to sexual intercourse. An added complication is exemplified by the situation in the United States where the age of consent varies from one state to another, the range being 12 to 18 years, although the usual age is 16. The latter applies generally in the UK, although only since 1885; before that it was 13 (Vinnika, 1989).

This last point may help us to see the matter in historical perspective. Part of the horror with which we regard the sexual abuse of children is due to the protected status we now accord to childhood in Western society. This special regard is not generally the case elsewhere in the world today (child prostitution is rife in some Asian countries, for example) and is a comparatively recent phenomenon in the UK (Aries, 1962). Raising the age of consent in Victorian England, just over one hundred years ago, was related to social concern about the large number of child prostitutes, there being tens of thousands of these in London alone (Pinchbeck and Hewitt, 1973). The sexual abuse of children in Western countries today is, therefore, in sharp contrast to our clearer view of the special, protected status of childhood, the definition of which, none the less, still poses problems.

Criteria used to define 'childhood' victims in sexual abuse research

3

vary from those in the pre-puberty category (e.g. Fritz, Stoll and Wagner, 1981) to those under 18 (e.g. Wyatt, 1985). On the other side, how does one define an abuser? Baker and Duncan (1985) give their definition of child sexual abuse as:

> A child (anyone under 16 years) is sexually abused when
> another person, who is sexually mature, involves the
> child in any activity which the other person expects to
> lead to their sexual arousal. (p. 458)

But someone who is 'sexually mature' can be legally a 'child'. A significant proportion of all sexual offences, including rape, is committed by those who are legally 'children' – in England and Wales approximately 18 per cent in 1988 (Home Office, 1989). The issue of 'consent' is relevant here. Sexual activity by mutual consent between post-pubertal children is undoubtedly common; without mutual consent it obviously amounts to 'abuse', but the distinction is not always easy to make. At the same time, a 15-year-old who engages in sexual activity with a 3-year-old would unquestionably be regarded as an abuser. Hence, the age-gap is an important factor in an operational definition of abuse.

When is something 'sexual'? It is most unambiguous when actual contact is involved. But adult nurturant behaviour may involve touching a child's genitals or other 'private' parts of the body. Here context and intent are defining factors. Much of reported sexual abuse is non-contact in character, i.e. exhibitionism, talking about sexual things in an erotic way, or showing the child pornographic material. Again interpretation is required. For example, an adult who allows a child to see him or her naked may or may not be behaving with sexual intent. Fraser's definition, given earlier, embodies what is probably the critical defining feature, namely that the act is for the 'sexual gratification of an adult'.

'Abuse' is largely defined by the child/adult or mature/immature dimensions. It does not need to involve violence or any other form of coercion. Violence is, in fact, not usually a part of child sexual abuse (Finkelhor *et al.*, 1990); seduction and enticement are the main means for the adult to achieve control. And those who physically abuse children are on the whole a different group from those who sexually abuse children (see Chapter 3). A key distinction is that whereas most physical abuse occurs *within* the family, sexual abuse occurs more often outside the family (Russell and Trainor, 1984).

As might be inferred from the preceding discussion, the issue of how much sexual abuse takes place is to a large extent a function of definition. Over-extensive definitions can make the problem appear unmanageable and distract attention away from those children most at risk from the more serious forms of abuse. Perhaps it should be emphasized that most children's experience of sexual abuse is of a single event of relatively minor character, as will be seen from the data presented in Chapter 2. A first task is to achieve an operational definition of: (1) the kinds of behaviour involved; and (2) the kinds of relationships which mean that they constitute abuse.

All conceivable forms of sexual activity happen between children and older or more mature persons. It is sufficient here to note the primary distinction usually made between *contact* and *non-contact* abuse. Non-contact abuse, as mentioned earlier, includes such things as exhibitionism and sexual invitations of one kind or another. Contact abuse ranges from sexual kissing to anal and vaginal intercourse and oral–genital sex. Where these latter occur with violence or other kinds of coercion they are regarded as the most extreme and intrusive forms of sexual abuse. However, trauma and distress for the child may be considerable even with the 'milder' kinds of abuse.

A widely used definition of the abusive relationship in age-differential terms is that devised by David Finkelhor and his associates at the University of New Hampshire (Finkelhor, 1979) namely:

- a sexual encounter between a child of 12 and under with a person of 19 or over;
- where the child is under 12 and the other person under 19 but at least 5 years older;
- where a child/adolescent is 13 to 16 years and the other person is at least 10 years older.

This compound definition makes a distinction between the pre-pubertal and post-pubertal child and by implication gives the adolescent child more responsibility for any sexual encounter. Unlike some other definitions used in research, it excludes *peer* sexual abuse. This is certainly more difficult to evaluate because most data are obtained by retrospective report (adults reporting on their experiences as children), and we are all prone to revalue our past experiences, particularly our 'mistakes', so that the past is not simply recalled but actively reconstructed in the present. Children engage in a good deal of 'sexual' activity with their age-peers (Goldman and Goldman, 1988), but any debate as to whether or not peer abuse constitutes child sexual abuse is just playing with words: if abuse occurs in any context it has to be recognized and dealt with.

In Chapter 2 we shall look at the scale of child sexual abuse by examining prevalence studies, which give some indication of how extensive the problem is in the population at large, and incidence studies, essentially those cases which are reported to medical, legal and a range of child care agencies. It is here that reporting bias is apparent, the most consistent being the under-reporting of the sexual abuse of boys. Chapter 3 briefly outlines the nature of child physical abuse and compares it with sexual abuse. In Chapter 4 we consider the question of evidence, mainly from medical and psychological standpoints: how does one recognize that abuse has occurred? Chapter 5 focuses on the short-term and long-term effects of sexual abuse in childhood, and underlines the importance of prevention: the main orientation of the book. Chapter 6 takes up this theme, examining in some detail those approaches which have been directed primarily at children, whilst Chapter 7 looks first at the perpetrators – who it is that we have to protect children against – and then considers ways in which other adults can support and safeguard children.

The greater part of the research to be reviewed is American. This is an area where US researchers have taken the lead; but can their findings be generalized? Those few studies that have been published in the UK show a remarkably similar picture, leading one to suspect that what is being uncovered may be characteristic of Western society as a whole. At the very least it seems reasonable to claim that US research data are likely to be a better guide than claims and assertions based on limited personal experience or on something even less impressive than that. Our concern has to be with *evidence* and evaluating its quality. In child sexual abuse, as in other areas of social concern, rhetoric and speculation are the least useful activities.

2
INCIDENCE AND PREVALENCE

This chapter is organized as a mixture of text and tables. The tables are more than just illustrative: they summarize and compare the major published studies of the incidence and prevalence of child sexual abuse. Not included are some unpublished studies which have proved difficult to obtain (mainly conference papers).

How large is the problem of the sexual abuse of children? How widespread is it in our sort of society? Both incidence and prevalence studies address these questions but, although the terms are sometimes used interchangeably, they represent quite different approaches (and the distinction is a useful one). *Prevalence* studies attempt to estimate the proportion of a population that has been sexually abused during childhood. *Incidence* studies, on the other hand, seek to estimate the number of new cases occurring in a given period of time, usually a year. In practice, incidence studies are of reported cases (from which estimates are often derived).

Public and professional awareness of sexual abuse is largely a phenomenon of the 1980s, particularly in the UK, although in the USA there was a significant recognition of the problem in the preceding decade. The escalation of this awareness is made dramatically clear in Table 2.1 (from Wild, 1986), which shows the number of children

Table 2.1. Numbers of referrals because of sexual abuse, physical abuse and neglect, 1976–85 (Leeds, England)

	1976	1977	1978	1979	1980	1981	1982	1983	1984	1985
Sexual abuse					3	5	7	9	50[a]	161[b]
Physical abuse and neglect	38[c]	88	86	86	110	189	188	208	231	332

[a] Abuse confirmed or considered to be probable in 30 cases.
[b] Abuse confirmed or considered to be probable in 106 cases.
[c] Cases of neglect not available for this year.

Source: Wild (1986).

referred to paediatricians in Leeds because of suspected abuse or neglect for the ten-year period 1976–1985. No children were referred because of possible sexual abuse before 1980, when there were just three cases: 2.6 per cent of all cases of suspected abuse. By 1985 the number had increased to 161 and the proportion to 34.8 per cent.

It is massive increments such as this which have led people to assert that reported or suspected cases are 'just the tip of the iceberg'. But before making astronomical extrapolations from the known to the unknown, two factors need to be borne in mind. First, the 'tip of the iceberg' of reported cases may not reflect the shape and distribution of what is out of sight; when incidence and prevalence data are compared we shall see how true this is. And second, prevalence studies represent a lifetime perspective – sixteen or seventeen years of childhood – while incidence figures are a one-year cross-section of the child population.

Too long a preamble without sight of the tabular summaries is likely to be confusing, so these are presented next. To make full sense of them, however, it will be necessary to refer back frequently.

APPARENT DISCREPANCIES IN THE DATA

From the prevalence summaries (Table 2.2) it is immediately apparent that no consistent picture emerges as to the 'true' prevalence rate of child sexual abuse. The reasons for the variation are not entirely clear but are likely to include differences in the populations sampled, the data-gathering techniques employed, and the preferred definition of sexual abuse (for example, contact/non-contact, the age-limits of 'childhood' or the definition of the abuser). Even if we exclude the two studies where the definition is somewhat imprecise (Fritz *et al.*, 1981; Kercher and McShane, 1984), the range is still 14.7 to 62 per cent for girls (average 32.6 per cent) and 6 to 30 per cent for boys (average 15.2 per cent). Note that this gives a ratio of roughly two girls to one boy. Is this same ratio reflected in incidence studies of reported cases?

On the basis of the prevalence studies we should expect approximately 70 per cent of reported cases to be girls and 30 per cent boys. If we cast our eye down Table 2.3 (incidence studies) we can see that this is far from the case. If the study by James *et al.* (1978) is excluded (which is particularly inadequate, and in any case reported *no* abuse of boys), the percentage range for girls is 81.8 to 91 per cent (average

86.9 per cent) and for boys 9 to 18.2 per cent (average 13.1 per cent). This yields a ratio of girls to boys of almost 7:1.

Police and social work data are rarely published in conventional form, although there is considerable inter-agency referral. Most of these incidence studies are therefore from medical sources. They relate almost entirely to contact abuse and usually the most severe forms. On the face of it the figures would seem to suggest that girls are more likely to experience these more severe forms of sexual abuse. However, what evidence there is from prevalence studies indicates that the reverse is true. Baker and Duncan (1985, p. 461) reported that boys were more likely than girls to experience contact abuse, and Goldman and Goldman (1988, p. 99) reported that boys were three times more likely to experience the most serious forms of abuse. Non-contact abuse by exhibitionists is almost entirely directed at girls, and Finkelhor (1979, p. 62) reported that 20 per cent of the female sample's sexual experiences were of this type.

The reasons for this bias in reported cases are unknown. It is known that boys are less likely than girls to report abuse (see Chapter 4). However, it is probable that, in the same way that child sexual abuse was not recognized because popular and professional assumptions ran counter to it, there is a general belief that boys are much less vulnerable to abuse than girls, this being one of a succession of myths which can only be overcome by a careful scrutiny of the evidence. The authors of one of the incidence studies (Spencer and Dunklee, 1986) point to the under-recognition of the sexual abuse of boys and show how referrals in this category to the San Diego Children's Hospital in California increased from one solitary case in 1979 to 5 per cent of the total in 1980, and to 14 per cent in 1984.

Another discrepancy apparent from a comparison of the tables is in the proportion of abusers who are female. In those few incidence studies where the sex of the abuser is reported, the proportion is extremely small (less than 3 per cent). A much more variable picture emerges from prevalence studies, although it is generally true that the great majority of abusers are male. Yet it is not true as some authors assert (e.g. Driver, 1989, p. 9) that women rarely sexually abuse children. This is another myth that has to be tackled on the evidence.

Where separate figures for boys and girls are given in prevalence studies, men are seen to be responsible for between 85.4 and 100 per cent of the abuse of girls (average 94.3 per cent) and for between 22 and 84 per cent of the abuse of boys (average 56.1 per cent). Two clear implications follow from this:

Table 2.2. Comparative analysis of prevalence studies: percentage of reported sexual abuse and sex of abusers

Study	Sample	Data collection[a]	Definition of abuse	Percentage reporting abuse	Sex of abusers (%) M	F	Notes
Landis (1956)	US college students (N = 1800)	SAQ	Contact and non-contact abuse	F = 35% M = 30%	80	20	Age definitions not clear
Gagnon (1965)	Non-random sample of US women (N = 1200)	PI	Contact and non-contact abuse	28% before age 13	[not given]		
Finkelhor (1979)	US college students (N = 796)	SAQ	Contact and non-contact abuse	F = 19% M = 9%	94 84	6 16	Response rate 92%
Fritz et al (1981)	US college students (N = 952)	SAQ	Contact abuse	F = 7.7% M = 3%	90 40	10 60	Definition of sexual abuse and age definition of victims not clear
Goodwin et al. (1982)	Non-random sample of US women (N = 500)	SAQ	Contact and non-contact abuse	24% before age 18	[not given]		Women were members of various voluntary organisations
Russell (1983)	Random sample of San Francisco women (N = 936)	PI	Contact and non-contact abuse	54% before age 18 48% before age 14	96	4	Response rate = 50%
Kercher and McShane (1984)	Random sample of Texas residents (N = 1056)	SAQ	Contact abuse	F = 11% M = 3%	[not given]		Questionnaires mailed to random sample of 2000; response rate 53%
Finkelhor (1984)	Random sample of Boston adults with children aged 6–14 (N = 521)	SAQ	Contact and non-contact abuse	F = 15% M = 6%	94	6	Response rate 74%

Baker and Duncan (1985)	Random sample of UK residents (N = 2019)	PI	Contact and non-contact abuse	F = 12% M = 8%	[not given: 'vast majority' male]		Compliance rate 87%
Nash and West (1985)	(i) 94 adult females on GP list (ii) 50 female college students UK	SAQ and PI (part sample)	Contact and non-contact abuse	(i) 42% (ii) 54%	99	1	(i) Response rate 42% (ii) Response rate 54%
Wyatt (1985)	Quota sample of Los Angeles women (N = 248)	PI	Contact and non-contact abuse	62% before age 18	Black: 97 White: 100	3 0	Refusal rate 45%
Fromuth and Burkhart (1987)	US male college students: (i) N = 253, Midwestern Univ. (ii) N = 329, Southeastern Univ.	SAQ	Contact and non-contact abuse	(i) 24% (ii) 20%	22 28	78 72	Data provided for more or less 'restrictive' definitions
Brière and Runtz (1988)	US female college students (N = 278)	SAQ	As Finkelhor (1979)	14.7%	85.4	14.6	
Goldman and Goldman (1988)	Australian higher education students (N = 991)	SAQ	As Finkelhor (1979)	F = 28% M = 9%	>90	<10	
Finkelhor et al. (1990)	US adults aged 18+ years (1481 F; 1145 M)	TI	Contact and non-contact abuse	F = 27% M = 16%	98 83	2 17	Refusal rate 24%

[a] SAQ, self-administered questionnaire; PI, personal interview; TI, telephone interview.

Table 2.3. Comparative analysis of incidence studies: sex of victims and sex of abusers

Study	Sample	Nature of abuse	Sex of victims (%) M	F	Sex of abusers (%) M	F	Notes
Jaffe *et al* (1975)	291 children (2–15 years); police records, Minneapolis	'Indecent liberties, sodomy, rape'	12	88	100	0	
James *et al.* (1978)	102 children (< 16 years) seen by sample of US physicians	Contact and non-contact abuse	0	100	?100	0	29% response rate to questionnaire
Tilelli *et al.* (1980)	130 children (2–16 years); hospital referrals, Minneapolis	'Indecent liberties, sodomy, rape'	13	87	[not given]		
Cantwell (1981)	287 children (average age 10.7 years); referred to multidisciplinary team, Denver	Contact abuse	14	86	97.4	2.6	
Rimsza and Niggemarn (1982)	311 children (0–17 years); hospital referrals, Phoenix	Contact abuse	14	86	100	0	

Table 2.3. Comparative analysis of incidence studies: sex of victims and sex of abusers (continued)

Study	Sample	Nature of abuse	Sex of victims (%)		Sex of abusers (%)		Notes
			M	F	M	F	
Mrazek et al. (1983)	218 children (0–15 years); seen by UK physicians	Primarily contact abuse	13.7	86.3	[not given]		39% response rate to mailed questionnaire; quality of data doubtful, e.g. sex of child not given in 35 cases.
De Jong et al. (1983)	566 children (6 months–16 years); referred to paediatric centre, Philadelphia	Contact abuse	18.2	81.8	99	1	Four female abusers, three of whom had a male accomplice
Spencer and Dunklee (1986)	1748 children (1–17 years); hospital referrals, San Diego	Contact abuse	9	91	[not given]		Authors note that percentage of boys referred was increasing
Reinhart (1987)	1152 children (0–17 years); referrals to medical centre, Sacramento	Contact and non-contact abuse	16.4	83.6	Boys: 96 Girls: not given	4	Study was mainly concerned with comparison of matched groups of M and F victims
Cupoli and Sewell (1988)	1059 children (0–16 years); hospital referrals, Florida	Severe contact abuse	11.2	88.8	97.7	2.3	

1 that boys are much more likely than girls to experience homosexual abuse.
2 that there are instances where the abuse of boys by women constitutes the majority of such incidents.

The first point may account for boys' greater tendency not to report abusive experiences, and the second requires some amplification because it runs counter to the conventional wisdom.

The first study to report a majority of female abusers was that of Fritz *et al.* (1981), who carried out a questionnaire survey with a population of 952 college students. Their questionnaire appears to have focused on the more serious forms of contact abuse occurring before the onset of puberty, which may account for the overall prevalence rates obtained (7.7 per cent for females, 4.8 per cent for males), amongst the lowest in the literature. But their findings challenged one stereotype of child abuse. They comment:

> Perhaps the most interesting finding is that the majority of
> the cases of male molestation (60%) were heterosexual in
> nature. The assumption has been that pre-adolescent
> males are nearly always molested by 'pathological'
> homosexuals. The preponderance of heterosexual
> molestation demonstrated by the data should seriously
> challenge this stereotype. (p. 57)

So much did the results run counter to those obtained in other studies in the early 1980s that Finkelhor (1984, p. 176) went so far as to suggest that 'it seems likely that the ... findings resulted from an unusual sample or an error in tabulation'.

However, a very similar picture emerged in a more recent and better-executed study by Fromuth and Burkhart (1987), using two similar populations of US male college students. Employing a range of definitions from 'least restrictive' (including all kinds of sexual abuse) to 'most restrictive' (limited to the more serious forms of sexual abuse), the authors reported prevalence rates of 24 per cent to 4 per cent in a Midwestern college sample ($N = 253$), and from 20 per cent to 4 per cent in a Southeastern college sample ($N = 329$). Contact abuse accounted for 9 per cent and 7 per cent, respectively, and in both samples the majority of the perpetrators was female (78 per cent and 72 per cent, respectively).

There are other myths challenged by the data. A very general assumption is that it is the development of secondary sexual characteristics which renders girls particularly vulnerable to abuse. But the evidence is quite clear that it is *pre-pubertal* girls who are most at risk. The four studies that provide average ages for both boys' and girls' abusive experiences are given in Table 2.4. It will be noted that girls

Table 2.4. Average age of first experience of sexual abuse (boys and girls)

Study	Boys (years)	Girls (years)
Baker and Duncan (1985, p. 459)	12.03	10.74
Goldman and Goldman (1988, p. 98)	10.3	9.8
Finkelhor (1984, p. 73)	11.4	9.7
Finkelhor (1979, p. 60)	11.2	10.2
Average	11.23	10.1

are consistently younger than boys in each study and the range of means across the different studies is only one year for girls as against two years for boys.

Landis (1956) presents his age distribution in terms of percentages for different age ranges and includes late adolescent/young adult experience of 'sexual deviates' – see the footnote to the original table reproduced here as Table 2.5. Note that the age ranges where the

Table 2.5. Percentages of 500 college men and women reporting experiences with adult sexual deviates at different ages

Age of subject at time of experience	Men[a] (%)	Women[b] (%)
4–6	1.0	9.6
7–8	4.0	18.6
9–10	6.0	13.7
11–12	14.0	11.3
13–14	21.0	15.1
15–16	19.0	11.7
17–18[c]	13.0	11.1
19 and over	20.0	7.5

[a] Based on 215 experiences.
[b] Based on 531 experiences.
[c] Experiences of subjects of 17 and over were included to show the changes in the nature of the deviate experiences with the increasing age of the subjects involved. Almost all the admitted experiences of boys of this age were with homosexuals; almost all those of girls of this age were with exhibitionists.
Source: Landis (1956).

largest number of incidents occur are 7–8 years for girls and 13–14 years for boys, and that before age 11 girls are more at risk, whereas after age 10 boys are more at risk. The mean differences in the other cited studies reflect a similar picture.

INTRAFAMILIAL ABUSE

Perhaps the most powerful belief, as general amongst professional workers as it is in the population at large, is that sexual abuse mainly occurs within the family. The strength of this professional assumption was demonstrated in the organization of the *National Study of the Incidence and Severity of Child Abuse and Neglect* conducted in 1979 and 1980, constituting one of the largest and most systematic attempts to collect data on cases of child abuse in the United States. Reviewing this study Finkelhor and Hotaling (1984) comment that:

> The legislation setting up the National Center for Child Abuse and Neglect and also mandating the NI study chose to define child abuse as acts committed by a 'parent substitute or other adult caretakers'.... Although this is an issue which has been substantially debated within the field, it is our own opinion that this is a very unfortunate limitation to put on the definition of child sexual abuse. *Child sexual abuse differs in this regard compared to almost all other forms of child abuse and neglect.* Adults who commit physical assaults or emotionally or physically neglect children are almost always parents and/or caretakers. Estimates vary, but from retrospective reports it seems probable that non-family abuse actually constitutes a *majority* of all abuse. (p. 26, emphasis added)

Presumably the assumption operating in the legislative programme that Finkelhor and Hotaling criticize was that sexual abuse was some kind of extension of other forms of physical abuse and neglect.

That the population of physically abused and neglected children is quite different from the population of sexually abused children is shown in a comparative epidemiological study (Jason *et al.*, 1982) of cases of abuse confirmed by the Georgia Department of Protective Services. Figure 2.1 gives the number of cases of physical and sexual abuse, by age, per 100,000 children. The age distributions are quite different in that physical abuse is more common pre-school (and most

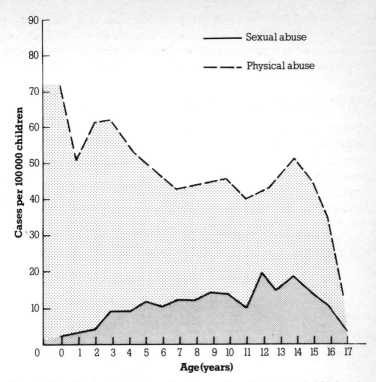

Figure 2.1. Rates by age of victim for confirmed cases of sexual and physical child abuse in Georgia, July to December 1979 (from Jason *et al.*, 1982).

frequent in the first year of life) while sexual abuse is more common in school-age children and peaks between 11 and 12 years. Other differences, as shown in this study, are as follows:

- 91 per cent of the sexually abused group were girls (although this percentage almost certainly under-represents the true proportion of abused boys); the proportions of boys and girls physically abused were approximately equal;
- 98 per cent of the known perpetrators of sexual abuse were male as against 56 per cent of the perpetrators of physical abuse;
- perpetrators of sexual abuse were more likely to be unknown or unrelated to the child (11 per cent versus 3 per cent) (but see the discussion that follows).

17

This epidemiological comparison is, of course, one form of incidence study and can be related to the incidence studies in Table 2.6. For those studies which report such data, the relationship of the child to the abuser is shown. From the figures it would appear that the overwhelming proportion of sexual abusers are known to their victims and that 'stranger danger' is not the main threat to children.

The category 'family' normally includes any relation and often includes co-habitees, etc. 'Acquaintances' are people known to the child but not related or living as part of the family; 'strangers' are those unknown to the child. In the 'family' category the range for these incidence studies is 23.7 to 71 per cent (average 45 per cent); the range for the 'acquaintances' category is 17 to 58.1 per cent (average 37.9 per cent); and for 'strangers' the range is 3 to 46.5 per cent (average 17 per cent).

However, when we look at prevalence studies, the data reveal significant differences (see Table 2.7). Here the average percentage for family abuse is 22.8 per cent (half the 'incidence' average); and while the average for 'acquaintance' abuse is almost exactly the same at 35.8 per cent, for 'stranger' abuse the average is 41.7 per cent, i.e. more than twice that shown by the incidence studies. This means that prevalence studies show the relative proportion of 'family' abusers as opposed to 'stranger' abusers to be approximately reversed. What reasons can be put forward for this discrepancy?

One possibility, running counter to what one might expect, is that intrafamilial abuse is more likely to be detected and reported. Finkelhor (1979) comments:

> Parents (mostly fathers and stepfathers) make up a large proportion of reported cases for several reasons. For one thing, they are conspicuous, create concern, and are thus likely to be pursued by those who know about them until they become official statistics. For another thing, although many families try to contain knowledge about parent–child incest, the dynamics are so volatile and the potential for conflict so great that they must be harder to hush up permanently than other kinds of children's sexual abuse. Thus even though the motivation for silence may be greater, the actual ability to contain it is less. (p. 140)

Since intrafamilial sexual abuse is often progressive in character, involving multiple incidents over a period of time, one can imagine that suppression of the true state of affairs becomes increasingly

Table 2.6. Comparative analysis of incidence studies: the relationship of victims to abusers

| Study | Sample | Relationship | | | Notes |
		Family (%)	Acquaintance (%)	Stranger (%)	
James et al. (1978)	102 F	71	17	12	
Tilelli et al. (1980)	113 F\n17 M	[76 'known']		24	
Cantwell (1981)	194 F\n32 M	64.5	19	16.5	'Family' category includes co-habitees
Rimsza and Niggemann (1982)	268 F\n43 M	42	40	18	Authors note that 25% of boys were assaulted by relatives and 10% by strangers
Mrazek et al. (1983)	158 F\n25 M\n35 sex not given	43	31	26	
De Jong et al. (1983)	463 F\n103 M	23.7	29.8	46.5	
Spencer and Dunklee (1986)	140 M	49	34	16	Relationship data not given for girls; 'stranger' category includes 4% 'unknown'
Reinhart (1987)	189 F\n189 M	43\n38	54\n58	3\n4	'Matched' female sample
Cupoli and Sewell (1988)	940 F\n119 M	30.5	58.1	11.4	In 198 cases details of perpetrator not available; 'family' includes co-habitee

Table 2.1. Comparative analysis of prevalence studies: the relationship of victims to abusers

Study	Sample	Relationship			Notes
		Family (%)	Acquaintance (%)	Stranger (%)	
Landis (1956)	1800	F M	33.8 30.5	65.2 68	500 questionnaires analysed of those reporting abuse
Gagnon (1965)	1200 F	15	26.5	58.5	
Finkelhor (1979)	530 F 266 M	43 17	33 53	24 30	
Russell (1983)	936 F	30	62	8	Includes peer abuse; recalculated data
Finkelhor (1984)	334 F 187 M	32	35	33	Figure for abuse by parents was 8% (of the 12% reporting abuse)
Nash and West (1985)	94 F 50 F(students)	18 17	33 16	49 67	No information available for 23 subjects
Wyatt (1985)	248 F	29 19	34 30	37 51	Afro-American White American
Baker and Duncan (1985)	2019 M and F	14	35	51	Girls more likely to be abused within family or by strangers; boys more likely to be abused by acquaintances
Goldman and Goldman (1988)	603 F 388 M	76		24	Relatives made up 35% of girls' experiences and 18% of boys'
Finkelhor et al. (1990)	1481 F 1145 M	29 11	50 49	21 40	

difficult. Another possibility is that since the incidence studies mainly report the more serious forms of contact abuse, intrafamilial abuse is predominantly of this nature. There are remarkably few studies bearing directly on this point. However, Russell (1983), in a particularly well-executed study, carried out a detailed analysis of intrafamilial and extrafamilial sexual abuse according to the following categories:

Very serious: vaginal, anal and oral intercourse
(completed or attempted); oral–genital sex.
Serious: genital fondling, simulated intercourse, digital
penetration.
Least serious: touching of clothed breasts or genitals, etc.

Her findings are summarized in Table 2.8. She concludes (p. 142): '... it is apparent that children who are sexually abused outside the family are abused in a significantly more serious manner'.

Table 2.8. Level of seriousness of sexual abuse: intrafamilial and extrafamilial

	Very serious (%)	Serious (%)	Least serious (%)
Intrafamilial	23	41	36
Extrafamilial	53	27	20

Source: Russell (1983).

Russell's finding is an important one because there has been much popular promotion of the belief that incest is rampant in our sort of society, e.g. Louise Armstrong's book *Kiss Daddy Goodnight* (1978), and the statement by the psychologists Risin and McNamara (1989, p. 179, para. 1) that 'incest is the most common form of sexual abuse'. The seriousness of 'classic' incest (sexual intercourse with a blood relative) is not to be underestimated, particularly as the long-term consequences for psychological disruption appear to be most marked in this category (see Chapter 5). But to overstate the case is to foster unhelpful sensationalism. Exaggeration discredits a case and may eventually promote a discounting reaction. What are the facts as shown by empirical research?

It is important to keep in mind the distinction between incest in the legal sense and what Goldman and Goldman (1984) describe as 'incestuous relationships' or 'intrafamilial sexuality', terms which cover *all* sexual experiences within the extended family. It is clear, from those studies that make the distinction, that girls are more likely to experience intrafamilial sexual abuse than boys. Finkelhor (1979) gives a percentage (of reported incidents) of 43 per cent for girls as against 17 per cent for boys. Baker and Duncan (1985) also report that girls are more likely to be abused by relatives. Goldman and Goldman (1988) give a figure, as a percentage of reported experiences, of 35 per cent for girls and 18 per cent for boys. For sexual intercourse with a blood relative the same authors give an overall percentage figure of 0.5, girls outnumbering boys by 2:1. For the same definition Baker and Duncan report a prevalence rate of 0.25 per cent.

Nash and West (1985) report three cases of actual or attempted sexual intercourse by a natural father and one by a stepfather in a total sample of 144 women. Finkelhor (1979) reported that five out of a sample of 530 women had had a 'sexual experience' with their natural father and two with their stepfather, i.e. rather more than 1 per cent of the total sample. Finkelhor points out that only 5 per cent of his sample had a stepfather and suggests that this indicates an increased risk for this category.

Russell (1984) found that 17 per cent of the women in her San Francisco sample with a stepfather had been sexually abused by him (8 per cent very seriously) as against 2.3 per cent abused by their natural father (0.5 per cent very seriously). The latter figure compares with those cited by Baker and Duncan (1985), and Goldman and Goldman (1988). On this basis it would seem reasonable to assume that 'classic' incest has a prevalence rate of around 1 in 200 women. Russell concludes that the incest taboo, although weaker than had once been supposed, is still operative. Indeed, the fact that the taboo exists is likely to be a factor in the serious psychological consequences for women of incestuous experiences in childhood.

3

THE RELATIONSHIP BETWEEN SEXUAL AND PHYSICAL ABUSE

Before going forward with the main topic of child sexual abuse we need to put it in the context of child abuse as a whole, and to take our bearings from the way in which the larger problem has been approached.

Concern about the conspicuously cruel and neglectful treatment of children developed only gradually during the nineteenth century, as a part of wider philanthropic movements and changed views of the nature of childhood. There is more than a note of irony in the fact that in both the UK and the USA, societies for the prevention of cruelty to animals were established before societies for the prevention of cruelty to children. Indeed, the first case seeking legal protection in the USA (a 10-year-old girl, starved and beaten by her adoptive parents) was brought by the Society for the Prevention of Cruelty to Animals in 1874 on the grounds that, being a member of the animal kingdom, she 'was entitled to at least the same justice as a common cur on the streets' (Bremmer, 1971, p. 185).

As the twentieth century progressed, the more flagrant forms of cruelty and neglect visibly diminished. The general well-being of children demonstrably improved: they were taller, heavier, less prone to disease, mortality rates declined, and so on. What was difficult to accept was that severe forms of physical and sexual abuse could co-exist with this vastly improved general treatment of children.

Our projection into awareness of the more concealed forms of child physical abuse (now universally acknowledged) bears a remarkable parallel to the more recent revelation of child sexual abuse. As noted in the first chapter, the 1980s have been the 'high-profile' decade for child sexual abuse, with limited awareness in the 1970s, and a state of almost complete non-awareness before that, despite isolated reports.

The physical abuse of children (and, in particular, of infants) was the revelation of the 1960s, the catalyst being the paper by Kempe *et al.* (1962) which identified 'the battered child syndrome'. But the evidence had been there, for attention and interpretation, for a long time. In 1946, for example, Caffey, a pediatric radiologist, published a clinical account of an association between subdural hematoma (bleeding underneath the fibrous membrane surrounding the brain – the *dura mater*) and fractures of the long bones in infants, based on observations he had been accumulating *since the early 1920s* (Caffey, 1946). He tentatively suggested that these might be due to accidental trauma, perhaps even inflicted by parents. The scepticism of colleagues had previously made him reluctant to publish his findings. In the same way that society found it hard to believe that caretakers or other adults should seek to have sexual relations with children, so it was incredible that parents could injure defenceless babies. Even if true, surely such things were rare, confined to a small number of seriously disturbed or psychopathic individuals?

Seven years elapsed before Silverman (1953) reported similar findings; observing that physical injury was the commonest bone 'disease' in infants, he suggested that careless handling by parents might be a cause. It was Wooley and Evans (1955) who suggested that the injuries were inflicted intentionally. Caffey (1957), after re-examining his earlier data, came to essentially the same conclusion. But note the timescale: more than a decade had elapsed before even informed professionals could agree as to the probability. From that date events moved only a little more swiftly, and Kempe and his colleagues in their key 1962 paper, cited above, refer to physicians' 'reluctance in believing that parents were guilty of abusing their children' (p. 24).

Kempe's paper forced the issue into public consciousness. Gelardo and Sanford (1987) comment that 'The spread of public response ... was astounding. In 1963 alone, 18 bills to protect the victims of child abuse were introduced in the US Congress and 11 of these were passed that year. Mandatory child abuse reporting laws were instituted in all 50 states by 1965' (pp. 137–8).

This credibility barrier is a reflection of the extent to which belief dictates evidence (or, at least, its interpretation). However, even when the 'facts' are acknowledged – in itself a difficult process, as this brief account shows – the interpretation of the evidence will be in terms of the levels and kinds of explanation available at that time. Thus, although the *fact* of child physical abuse was acknowledged almost overnight, our way of thinking about the subject changed considerably over the next twenty years.

How to explain the behaviour of parents who physically abused their children in a serious fashion? The ready-made explanations of the early 1960s were primarily psychiatric, i.e. presuming that 'abnormal' parenting behaviour was the outcome of abnormal psychological development. But as large-scale data began to be accumulated during that decade, via the newly established reporting procedures, different dimensions of the problem emerged. A particularly influential large-scale study was that by Gil (1970), who analysed all the reports of child physical abuse and neglect notified in the United States during 1967 and 1968: over 20,000 cases. He found that social disadvantage – unemployment, poverty, large family size, unsettled housing, and so on – were major contributory factors. Not that these were sufficient explanations; the majority of parents experiencing these difficulties did *not* abuse their children.

Clearly child physical abuse had to be seen as part of a *system* of interacting elements, a range of predisposing conditions in the individuals and in the environment which could summate to produce the abuse. This multifactor way of viewing the problem, an *ecological* perspective, was most clearly proposed in Garbarino's (1977) paper 'The human ecology of maltreatment: A conceptual model for research'. This ecological model became increasingly influential during the 1980s and attracts much current interest because of its implications for preventive action (e.g. Cotterill, 1988). Because there is a much weaker association with social disadvantage, it seems unlikely that an ecological analysis would add much to the prevention of child *sexual* abuse. But it has to be noted that there is no research directly bearing on this issue.

CHILD SEXUAL ABUSE COMPARED WITH CHILD PHYSICAL ABUSE

The professional response to child sexual abuse came from a system (in medicine and social work) conditioned by what was known about child physical abuse, i.e. that it was associated with indices of social deprivation and that it occurred, almost exclusively, within the family. There was, therefore, an in-built bias, not just in people's minds but in the way the system operated. The analysis of all US reporting data on child abuse and neglect for the period 1976–82 carried out by the American Humane Association (Russell and Trainor, 1984) casts some light on the operation of this process. For example, over the seven-year period, the percentage of families of sexually abused children receiving public assistance declined from 39.8 to 29.3 per cent, although there was no similar decline in families where other forms of abuse were reported (stable at around 45 per cent). The authors comment (p. 35) that the 'trend perhaps indicates that a new population of sexual abuse families is being identified – one that is less tied to public welfare bureaucracy' and that 'another new population of sexual abuse victims is now being identified – one that is less visible to health professionals ...'. This bias is probably reflected in the incidence studies of reported cases of child sexual abuse discussed in the previous chapter and is a factor that has to be borne in mind in evaluating 'official' statistics.

Although not on the same scale as the US statistics reported by Russell and Trainor, a UK study by Creighton (1985) provides information on 6,532 children placed on child abuse registers maintained by the National Society for the Prevention of Cruelty to Children in England for approximately the same period as the US study.

Both studies find that the average age of physically abused children is very much lower than the average age of sexually abused children. And both report roughly equal numbers of both sexes in physical abuse victims, but a ratio of around 5 : 1 (girls to boys) in sexual abuse victims (in line with the incidence studies reported in the last chapter, but see the discussion on that point).

Creighton reports that approximately equal numbers of natural mothers and fathers were implicated in child physical abuse (28.4 per cent and 28.9 per cent respectively), with 19.1 per cent of cases being undetermined and 17.1 per cent being by parent substitutes. Russell and Trainor, in their much larger study, report a preponderance of female perpetrators in cases of child physical abuse (60.8 per cent) as against 21 per cent in cases of child sexual abuse.

Creighton identifies a number of characteristics of abusive families which have been frequently replicated:

- only around half of the children were living with both natural parents (52.8 per cent in 1977, decreasing to 44 per cent in 1982);
- 35.3 per cent of the mothers were aged less than 20 at the time of the child's birth (the national average being 10.7 per cent for manual social classes);
- abused children were nearly three times as likely to be living in families with four or more children;
- male caretakers were more likely to be unemployed (35 per cent in 1977, rising to 58.2 per cent in 1982,

compared with a national trend of 6 to 14.4 per cent over the same period).

She concludes that in adverse economic circumstances 'the young, poorly educated parents of large families with few skills to offer in the job market are most at risk . . . . The children of such parents are over-represented on child abuse registers' (p. 447).

One feature of families vulnerable to child physical abuse (and which distinguishes them from families where children are liable to be sexually abused) is a preponderance of female single parents. Russell and Trainor report a percentage of 21.3 for child sexual abuse (close to the 17 per cent national average) but twice that figure for child physical abuse families (40.8 per cent).

What is not apparent from these official statistics is *why* single parents (predominantly women) are more likely to physically abuse their children. Is it due to

- the supposed stress of bringing up a child single-handed?
- associated poverty and deprivation?
- the age of the caretaker (likely to be young)?

Gelles (1989) reports on a national random survey of 6,000 households in the USA which investigated the levels of violence parents used towards their children. He found that associated poverty was the key factor in child physical abuse in female single-parent families, but that income was unrelated to the high level of violence in *male* single-parent families (of which there were far fewer). His analysis is derived from one of the few *prevalence* studies of child physical abuse (Straus and Gelles, 1986). Prevalence studies are much commoner in research on sexual abuse, where they are almost all *retrospective* studies of adult subjects.

In the investigation of child physical abuse much greater reliance has been placed on official statistics of reported cases, e.g. the study by Gil (1970) cited above. The sheer size of the populations involved commands respect. Russell and Trainor's 1984 report for the American Humane Association is an analysis of approximately one and a quarter million cases. But this is still only an analysis of those detected and reported, and large-scale studies can mean large-scale biases. As Gelles (1989) points out (p. 492): 'Official report data, while offering the advantages of larger sample size, confound the factors associated with abuse with those factors related to being reported, either correctly or incorrectly, to official agencies.'

Gelles' comment focuses on the important distinction between whether or not the cases are *known* to relevant professionals, and whether they are *reported*. The US central agency, the National Center on Child Abuse and Neglect (NCCAN), surveyed the reporting/non-reporting process (U.S. Department of Health and Human Services, 1981). Using data from a stratified random sample of 26 counties in 10 states they examined cases detected by relevant professionals (police, doctors, and so on) and compared those reported with those not reported. They found that two-thirds of such cases were *not* reported to the child protection agencies (although it was mandatory to do so). This discovery was important in itself but a key question was whether biases were apparent in those cases 'selected' for report. Contrary to what might have been expected, there was no reporting bias along lines of race; there was some under-reporting of more affluent families – significant because it is most likely to relate to sexual abuse; and a marked bias in favour of reporting younger children. Russell and Trainor (1984, p. 15) conclude that 'except for age bias, official reporting statistics provide reasonably good information both about the cases processed by CPS agencies as well as the nature of child maltreatment' – to which should be added – *'in so far as it is known to relevant professionals'*.

Reporting is distinct from detection; and detection is distinct from true prevalence. The history of professional awareness of child abuse clearly demonstrates that detection depends to a large extent on the perception of the nature of the problem. Because physical abuse was evidently something *parents* did to children, and was strongly associated with social disadvantage, it is likely that professional expectations were that sexual abuse was somewhat similar.

The apparent bias in professional procedures for the reporting of parental sexual abuse was noted in the previous chapter: despite this the distinctive character of child sexual abuse asserts itself. Russell and Trainor (1984, p. 32) comment: 'The profile of maltreatment experienced by sexual abuse victims is significantly different from the profile experienced by all child abuse and neglect victims ... beside the sexual maltreatment itself, there is relatively little additional maltreatment.... Thus, this subgroup may be viewed as relatively distinct.'

As was noted in Chapter 1 (Finkelhor *et al.*, 1990), sexual abuse is not characterized by the use of force, except in a small minority of cases. The question remains, in any case, whether the physical abuse associated with sexual abuse is like other forms of physical abuse of children or is in a special category, e.g. as part of sexual assault.

The answer is not clear-cut. A recent paper by Hobbs and Wynne (1990) reports on the cases of 130 children identified in Leeds, England, over the four-year period 1985–88. The 77 girls and 53 boys, with mean ages of 5.7 years and 6.8 years respectively, were diagnosed as having been both sexually and physically abused. The data in this study are not clear but suggest that sexual abuse can co-exist with physical abuse that is not directly related, but that some physical abuse *is* directly related to sexual abuse. The authors comment: 'In many cases the pattern of physical abuse is indistinguishable from the classical cases described in the literature over many years. In others, the presence of burns, grasp or pinch marks, or scratches around the lower body, genitalia, anus, thighs, knees, or buttocks would make one think of the possibility of a sexual motivation behind the assault' (p. 426).

IS CHILD ABUSE INCREASING?

Studies such as the foregoing make sobering reading. Is it true that we are dealing with an escalating epidemic of child abuse? The data presented by the NSPCC in the UK and NCCAN in the USA certainly show increasing numbers of children *reported*. But does this mean that child abuse, despite public concern and professional action, is actually increasing? A part answer comes from changes in the pattern of abusive incidents.

Creighton (1985), referring to statistics for the years 1977 to 1982 observes: 'In contrast to the overall increase in reported physical injury ... there was a decrease in fatal or serious injury. Of the physically injured children, 16.8 per cent had fatal or serious injuries in 1977, but only 10.1 per cent in 1982. Less than 1 per cent of the physical injuries were fatal. The majority of the abused children received soft tissue injuries only. The reported re-injury rate has also fallen. Of the children registered in 1977, 11.2 per cent were re-injured or re-abused in the year following registration, but only 6.9 per cent of those registered in 1982' (p. 443).

It is, of course, impossible to allocate precise causes to these changing trends but professional alertness and intervention, in conjunction with raised public awareness, are the likely candidates. Paradoxically the same causes are likely to be the reasons for the overall *increase* in the number of cases reported. Straus and Gelles (1986), referring to the American scene, point out that two main factors could account for the increase in the officially reported rate when the true incidence could actually be *declining*; the first factor being that all states in the USA now have compulsory child abuse reporting laws, so that previously unreported cases come to the attention of child welfare services. They add:

> The second factor is much more fundamental. Without it, the reporting system would not work even to the extent that it now operates. This is the fact that new standards are evolving in respect to how much violence parents can use in child-rearing. . . .
>
> Changed standards are also the real force behind the child abuse reporting laws. Were it not for these changing standards, the reporting laws would not have been enacted; or, if enacted, they would tend to be ignored. (pp. 466–7)

Straus and Gelles's study, comparing levels of family violence in two national surveys carried out in 1975 and 1985, reports a marked reduction, especially in the most severe forms of physical punishment, over that decade. Parents still commonly hit their children but it is evidently less widely sanctioned and no longer regarded as being as 'normal', or even desirable, as it once was. The virtual abolition of corporal punishment in UK schools over the past fifteen years parallels this trend. Treatment once considered acceptable becomes unacceptable and the more severe forms of maltreatment are thrown into sharper relief. The whole process shows the possibility of widespread shifts in the moral climate, with important consequences for the prevalence and seriousness of social problems. It has implications for what might happen as a result of greater societal awareness of, and sensitivity to, child *sexual* abuse.

It may be too early to look for such effects but a recent paper by Bagley (1990) is the first to suggest that the *real* prevalence of child sexual abuse may be declining. Bagley carried out a retrospective-report survey of 750 women aged 18 to 27 years in Calgary, Alberta, during 1988–89. The women constituted a stratified random sample of ten age cohorts of approximately 75 each. Those aged 18 and 19 reported significantly less contact abuse up to age 16 than those aged 20 to 27 years. Previous studies (e.g. Nash and West, 1985) have always shown the reverse relationship, with older women tending to report less abuse in childhood.

In Bagley's study decreased prevalence was associated with familiarity with the topic via the media. He argues that a climate of greater publicity and awareness of ways of avoiding or stopping such abuse may be factors in an actual decline. Publicity, in any case, presumably affects potential abusers as well as potential victims.

The purpose of this chapter has been to highlight the major distinctions between child sexual abuse and child physical abuse and to consider what lessons can be drawn from our longer-standing awareness of the latter. It is evident that an accurate recognition of such problems does not emerge immediately; but is indispensable for mobilizing effective public opinion as well as constructing effective forms of intervention. In the next chapter, returning to our main theme, we consider how *evidence* of sexual abuse is obtained: a considerably more difficult task than in the case of physical abuse.

4

THE EVIDENCE FACTOR

Shifting the focus now from large-scale surveys to the individual child, we need to ask: 'How do we *know* when a child has been sexually abused?'

The simplest answer (and the best evidence) is that the child tells someone, more or less spontaneously. This is usually referred to as *disclosure*. But children often don't tell anyone, or what they say may be allusive or incomplete. Contrary to popular assumption, such spontaneous disclosures are rarely fabrications (less than 1 per cent in a review of various studies by Goodwin *et al.*, 1979). *Interview* evidence can be less reliable unless expertly handled – the interviewer needs to facilitate disclosure rather than extract it. Children, in particular, are vulnerable to suggestion or leading questions, although these are usually considered admissible once the basic character of the evidence has been disclosed (Jones and McQuiston, 1988, p. 35).

Evidence of emotional disturbance or other presumed psychological developmental abnormalities (e.g. precocious knowledge of sex) – referred to as *psychological indicators* – are often cited, but, as we shall see, none of them can safely be regarded as specific to sexual abuse, and may not be all that unusual in the population at large. A final strand of direct evidence is that derived from *medical assessment*. Although this might be thought definitive, in most cases there are no physical findings and when physical evidence is present there are often problems in evaluating it.

Distinct from the kind of evidence that focuses on the individual is the evaluation of other *risk factors*: those personal circumstances which mean that a child is more likely (in an actuarial sense) to experience sexual abuse.

These different kinds of evidence will now be analysed in more detail with reference to research findings.

DISCLOSURE

The British Crime Survey carried out in 1981 (Home Office, 1983) found that sex crimes in general were the least likely to be reported: less than 10 per cent across all age ranges. Kutchinsky (1971) – cited in Swift (1979) – found that three times as many female as male victims of sex crimes reported the incident to the police. This compares with a ratio of reporting given by the sample in Landis's study of a student population (Landis, 1956). In this retrospective study of child sexual abuse, 43 per cent of the girls and 16.5 per cent of the boys said that they had told their parents of the incidents. Landis comments:

> It is interesting that girls do not seem to tell their parents about the more serious experiences; 46 per cent of those exposed to exhibitionists told their parents; in cases of sexual touching or fondling, 36 per cent of those exposed told; in attempts at coitus, 28.8 per cent told; and in homosexual approaches, 12.5 per cent of those exposed told. (p. 98)

Since it is usually the case that perpetrators are men, offences against boys are predominantly homosexual in character. As we noted in the previous chapter, it is possible that society's attitude to homosexuality inhibits disclosure. It should be noted that, in the data given by Landis above, girls who experienced homosexual advances had an overall reporting rate very similar to boys.

In another retrospective study of childhood abusive incidents Gagnon (1965) found that only in 6 per cent of the incidents mentioned by his subjects could they remember their being reported to the police. And for 21 per cent of the incidents, the report to the interviewer was the first time that the subject had ever told anyone.

It is interesting to compare these comparatively 'old' data with Russell's more recent study of 930 adult women in San Francisco (Russell, 1983) in which she found, for a different generation of women, a very similar level of reporting to the police (2 per cent in cases of intrafamilial sexual abuse, 6 per cent in cases of extrafamilial abuse). Russell does not give any data on the initial disclosure by her subjects.

Even when children do report the incidents, initial disclosure is often delayed. In one survey 49 per cent of the abused children delayed reporting for longer than 24 hours, and 22 per cent told only after multiple episodes (De Jong *et al.*, 1983). Another survey found that 55 per cent delayed reporting for longer than 72 hours and 30 per cent only after multiple episodes (Rimsza and Niggemann, 1982). These 'delay' factors have important implications for obtaining medical evidence, since after 72 hours many of the physical signs will have disappeared.

Very little is known, in any systematic fashion, about the ways in which perpetrators seek to maintain a child's silence. In any case, it is unlikely to be as simple as that. As the differential levels of reporting given above indicate, children often sense that their experiences are something that cannot be talked about. One of the significant outcomes of prevention programmes (see Chapter 6) is that they appear to enable children to disclose their experiences, presumably because such programmes make the subject 'permissible' and believable.

INTERVIEW EVIDENCE

The issue of the credibility of children's reports of sexual abuse is considered under this heading but applies equally to the previous one. Faller (1988), commenting on the amount of attention given to the issue of whether children lie about sexual abuse, says, 'In large part, the preoccupation with this issue has its origin in the difficulty many people continue to experience in believing that adults can choose to be sexual with children' (p. 389).

It is the case, however, that the appraisal of whether children's reports are true often depends on 'clinical judgement' which focuses on three aspects of the child's behaviour in the interview situation:

- the child's ability to provide circumstantial detail of the context of the abuse;
- the child's description or demonstration (with, for example, anatomical dolls) of the sexual activities;
- the child's emotional state.

Faller (1988) examined 103 cases of abuse where the perpetrator had made a full or partial confession, and assessed the presence or absence of these supposed criteria of 'true' accounts in the child interviews. Approximately 80 per cent of the children (average age 9 years) met the three criteria in their accounts, although this was less true of boys than of girls. Young children (under 6 years) had a particular difficulty in describing the context of the abuse and their account was generally more incomplete.

Interviews are usually carried out when there is already some professional suspicion that sexual abuse has occurred (e.g. medical evidence, reports of social workers). This can be treacherous ground for the interviewer and can lead to the over-interpretation of ambiguous statements, or of the child's play or drawings. Howitt (1990) reports a case where a psychologist inferred that abuse had taken place from the content of a story the child had written. The child's story turned out to be derived from a children's book she had recently read.

PSYCHOLOGICAL INDICATORS

Examples of the kind of psychological/psychiatric indicators that are considered to have possible clinical significance are given in Table 4.1 (from Indest, 1989). As the author states, these *may* mask sexual

Table 4.1. Emotional and mental manifestations that may mask sexual abuse

Infants and toddlers:	Adolescents:
Sleep disturbances	Suicidal ideation and gestures
Irritability	Psychogenic pains
Feeding problems	Fright and confusion
Altered levels of activity	Anger and acting out
Excess physical aggression	Impulsiveness
Hyperactivity	Deteriorating school performance
	Guilt feelings
School-age children:	Depression
Anxieties	Mental immaturity
Nightmares	Psychoses
Impulsive behaviour	Schizophrenia
Excess physical aggression	
Psychogenic pains	
Lethargy	
Withdrawn attitude	
Seizures	
Deteriorating school performance	
Introversion	
Sleep disturbances	
Behavioral problems	

Source: Indest (1989).

abuse, but the link is a tenuous one. Whilst many of the behaviours could be considered manifestations of psychological disturbance, some are so common as to be regarded as not even abnormal in children, let alone diagnostic of a specific causation. For this reason psychological 'indicators' can never be used in isolation, since children's responses are so varied. Sink (1988) notes that attempts to identify a *sexually abused child syndrome* are

> fraught with problems, most of them stemming from the

fact that sexual abuse, although used as a global term,
refers to broadly heterogeneous events that differ
markedly in their severity and meaning for the children
who are abused. Add the range of factors which mediate
the response to the abuse (the child's resiliency and
coping, the available social supports, and the family's
response to abuse) and one sees widely varied
symptoms among victims. (p. 130)

She concludes:

> *with the exception of precocious and atypical sexualizing*
> *behaviours in some children, the patterns observed are*
> *not specific to abused children.* (p. 131; emphasis added)

Sink herself puts forward a four-level model of 'symptomatology',
moving from the most certain at level 1 to the least certain at level 4
(Table 4.2). Hence those behaviours which are most open to interpretation are rated as least certain.

MEDICAL ASSESSMENT

If psychological indicators are, in the main, ambiguous or non-specific, it might be thought that medical evidence, i.e. physical signs, would be more certain. The assumptions here are so powerful that the nature of medical evidence needs to be considered in some detail, especially as the nature of the evidence and the techniques employed are little known to the layman or, indeed, to many professionals with an interest in child sexual abuse. In the UK the issue of the status of these kinds of finding was brought into sharp focus by what is generally referred to as the Cleveland affair, a matter which led to the setting up of an inquiry conducted by a High Court judge (DHSS, 1988).

In 1986 the *Lancet* published a paper entitled 'Buggery in childhood – a common syndrome of child abuse' (Hobbs and Wynne, 1986). The authors detailed the kind of injuries to the anus and the surrounding area which might be found in such cases. They also described a characteristic – reflex anal dilation – which *in the absence of other physical evidence* might indicate that the child had been penetrated anally. Reflex anal dilation is elicited by separating the buttocks, usually with the child in the knee to elbow position; if dilation occurs, after a few seconds the anal canal opens and allows a view of the rectum. Finkel (1989) observes that 'an abnormal response to the

Table 4.2. Levels of symptomatology of child sexual abuse

Level	Symptoms

1. Direct communication	Verbal disclosure
	  detailed in age-appropriate
	  language
	  affect-appropriate contextual
	  statements
	Demonstration on sexually
	  anatomically correct dolls
	Physical corroboration

2. Indirect communication	Ambiguous, contextual statements Sexualized play Sexualized behaviour Atypical response to sexual stimuli Sexualized response to projective tests Retraction of prior disclosure

3. Acute traumatic symptomatology	Post-traumatic play (nonsexualized)
	  themes: terror, entrapment, danger,
	  repetition
	Post-traumatic symptomatology
	  fearfulness
	  mood lability
	  separation distress
	  enuresis/encopresis
	  sleep disorder
	  change in social/academic
	  functioning

4. Cumulative stress symptomatology	Chronic behavioural maladaption
	  conduct disorder
	  psychosomatic disorder
	  dissociative reactions
	  phobias
	  depression/suicidal ideation

Source: Sink (1988).

separation of the buttocks is the spontaneous dilation of the anus greater than 15 mm'. However, it must be emphasized that there is a complete lack of 'normal' baseline data, i.e. the frequency of this characteristic in children who have not been abused. As we shall see below, the lack of comparative 'normal' data applies to other physical measures.

In the Cleveland area (the South Tees Health District) during a period of a few months the paediatricians involved (using Hobbs and Wynne's guidelines) diagnosed sexual abuse in some 125 children – both male and female – in some cases on no other evidence whatsoever except 'abnormal' anal findings. The concern and disagreement provoked by the affair led to the statutory inquiry previously cited. The published report, unlike many such documents, makes fascinating reading, not because of its sensational features – which the report puts into perspective – but because of the process of well-intentioned error it reveals, and the soundness of the recommendations it makes. The report lays emphasis on the need for multi-disciplinary assessment and for care and caution in obtaining and evaluating especially medical and interview findings.

A direct result of the Cleveland Inquiry has been a considerable tightening up of the conduct and scope of medical examinations, especially the scrupulous recording of the results. Steiner and Taylor (1988) provide a comprehensive plan for such an examination of the ano-genital area and the recording of findings. Physical evidence of sexual abuse other than rectal or vaginal penetration is rarely available. As Finkel (1989) has pointed out: 'Superficial trauma to the genitalia and anus can heal without residual in less than 72 hours. More serious trauma heals with the formation of scar tissue and will be apparent long after the event' (p. 1147).

In girls, where it is suspected that they have been the victims of vaginal penetration, a careful examination of the hymen and the size of the vaginal opening is usually considered necessary. However, as Geddis (1989) comments:

> attempts have been made to correlate allegations of
> sexual abuse with measurements of vaginal opening size.
> Such attempts have been hampered by the startling
> discovery that data on normal variations at different ages
> are not available. Some authors have reported that, in the
> absence of a clear history of accidental trauma, a finding
> of a vaginal opening of greater than 4 mm is strong
> supportive evidence of sexual abuse.

He continues:

> it has to be acknowledged that at this time it is not
> possible to state definitively that any one specific genital
> measurement is conclusive evidence that child sexual
> abuse has or has not occurred. The same can be said of
> specific anal findings. (p. 99)

A study by Emans *et al.* (1987) of genital signs in sexually abused girls, normal children, and children with a variety of genital complaints showed that there was considerable overlap.

Even when cases of sexual abuse are considered legally proven (a tough criterion), corroborating physical evidence is usually not available. In a recent study by De Jong and Rose (1989) of 39 cases where there was conviction of the perpetrator, only nine had physical evidence and the conviction rate was, in fact, higher for those cases without it (94 per cent as against 69 per cent: a difference significant at the 10 per cent level, using the chi-squared test). The corollary of this is that children's verbal testimony (in whatever context) carries considerable weight. De Jong and Rose comment: 'not only did judges and juries conclude that sexual contact with penetration could occur without leaving physical evidence, the perpetrators in nearly a third of the cases admitted to these acts in the absence of physical evidence' (p. 1025). Similar low levels of physical signs in children where there was a high probability of sexual abuse are given elsewhere (for example, Herbert (1987) reports 29 per cent in a sample of 55 children).

RISK FACTORS

Risk factors are different from all the preceding categories in that they are not *diagnostic* as such but indicate, in an actuarial sense, the probability that other signs might be valid. These factors are those social and economic variables that might place a child at greater risk of sexual abuse. Finkelhor (1980) identifies eight such variables:

- living in a family with a stepfather;
- having lived at some time without the mother;
- not being close to the mother;
- having a mother who never finished high school;
- having a sexually punitive mother;
- having no physical affection from the father;
- living in a family with an income of less than $10,000 per year;
- having two friends or fewer.

Finkelhor's list is based on US data but the factors he identifies are broad. Of these the first is likely to be the most valid (as we saw from Russell's research findings (Russell, 1984) cited earlier). What is particularly interesting about this list is the significance it attaches to the quality of the child's relationship with the mother, implying that a good relationship affords protection on the one hand and the reduction of the child's emotional vulnerability on the other. It would appear that many molesters are skilful in assessing the emotional needs of vulnerable children and exploiting them in a sexual way.

5

THE EFFECTS OF ABUSE

For most people the taboo against adults engaging in any kind of sexual activity with children is so strong that no further reason is required for regarding such behaviour as a very serious offence. But it still remains relevant to ask whether such experiences actually do children any harm in the short or the long term.

The perhaps surprising answer appears to be that for the great majority of children there are no lasting effects, and quite often no immediate effects either. However, in seeking to establish cause-and-effect relationships we are into a familiar methodological problem. Immediate consequences are fairly easy to determine: they are instantaneous and direct in their character. Long-term outcomes are necessarily more speculative, even when the causal association appears to make sense. This is particularly true when the structure of a research investigation, in effect, 'leads' the adult subjects to make such an association between abusive incidents in the past and their current psychological state.

Gagnon (1965) sums up the problem for researchers:

> As in all retrospective studies that relate early experiences to the current state of the individual, it is not possible to trace the current condition in a direct causal line from the previous condition. Data are lacking on the larger aspects of these individuals' lives that might in fact have been the precipitating factors in poor adult adjustment. Moreover, these factors may well have not been sexual in nature, and yet they may have had an effect on the sexual dimension of the personality and behaviour. (p. 188)

It is not enough to demonstrate, for example, that women who have been abused as children are more likely to show signs of general psychological disturbance or sexual maladjustment. For example, Nash and West (1985), in a comparison of women who had or had not been abused in childhood, found that the women in the abused group were more likely to report sexual dysfunction and less likely to engage in sexual activity. But that does not prove that the earlier experiences caused the problems of adult adjustment.

This is true even when the 'deviance' or 'disorder' is very marked. A number of studies have shown high proportions of abusive childhood experiences amongst, for example, female prostitutes (James and Meyerdring, 1977) or female psychiatric referrals (Rosenfeld, 1979; Sheldon, 1988; Craine *et al.*, 1988), although the authors of these studies are well aware of the methodological snares. Craine *et al.* state: 'an alternative implication is that the abuse may be part of the generally unstable environment in which many patients lived their early years, and that patients' experience of this instability may have resulted in hospitalization' (p. 303). And James and Meyerdring, in tackling the issue, comment:

> It is not possible ... to conclude that, because our sample population of 'deviant' women were disproportionately victims of rape and incest, these sexual abuses were therefore the cause of deviance. On the other hand, the overfrequent victimization of these women, particularly in youth and childhood, is a fact – just as their status as 'deviants' is a fact – and should not be lightly dismissed. (p. 40)

However, before going on to tease out these more tenuous long-term associations we need to consider the reactions and experiences of children immediately following abusive incidents. If there *is* a causal relationship, then this is the beginning of the chain.

INITIAL REACTIONS

We have to distinguish between the initial reactions of the *child* and the initial reactions of caretaking adults – which presumably affect the outcomes for the child to some extent. Nash and West (1985), who studied two groups of abused women, report that the initial reactions of both groups were *mainly* negative but that 31 per cent of one group and 50 per cent of the other reported *some* positive feeling. Finkelhor (1979), reporting on the females in his sample, found that 58 per cent of the girls reacted with fear, 26 per cent with shock, while only 8 per cent reported pleasure. Goldman and Goldman (1988), using Finkelhor's methodology with a similar population in Australia, report very similar data but also show significant sex differences (see Table 5.1) – a point to be taken up later. Landis, in his much earlier study (Landis, 1956), presented a similar picture of initial reactions (p. 98) and also a 'recovery' timetable (reproduced here as Table 5.2) which, with the necessary cautions, can be seen as a bridge between initial and later reactions.

Quite separate from the child's own first reactions are the responses of adults to the child's disclosures. These would seem often to be extremely unhelpful, and sometimes traumatic in themselves. Landis reports (pp. 99–100) that over 5 per cent of the girls who told their parents were more frightened by their reactions than by the experiences themselves. Likewise, Gagnon found that some of the women in his study, neutral about the incident, became horrified and upset because of the extreme character of the parental response to their report (Gagnon, 1965, p. 184). The preponderance of unhelpful reactions is very marked in the 'initial reactions' table offered by Nash and West (1985) (Table 5.3). As an example, the verbatim recollection of one family's reaction is quoted below.

> My mother was hysterical for days. She cried and cried. My father was furious and went around shouting.... I felt it was all my fault – that I was the cause of my mother's distress.... My mother took me and asked me if he had ever touched me and what he'd done to me. At first I denied it and then I said he had. Then they put me into the spare bed until the doctor came. I was perfectly well and couldn't understand why the doctor was coming. Mother took me to bed and cried and cried and asked me to tell her how often it had happened and in the end I said a dozen times. Then the doctor came and (this went on over two or three days) and the doctor examined me on the dining table. He looked at me and confirmed that I was still a virgin. My parents heaved a sigh of relief then they told me never to talk to anyone about it, and it was never mentioned again. ... I think my parents handled it appallingly. ... They told me never to tell anyone again. If only they'd been able to talk about sex and explain that adult sex is not like that. (p. 62)

Whilst this is likely to be an extreme instance it probably reflects

Table 5.1. Reactions of children at the time to sexual abuse by older persons

	Girls (N=188)	Boys (N=40)
	%	%
Fear	43	24
Shock	25	6
Surprise	16	32
Interest	12	21
Pleasure	5	18
Negative reaction	68	30

Source: Goldman and Goldman (1988).

Table 5.2. Time required to recover from emotional shock of sex deviate experiences as reported by 500 college students

Time required	Men[a] (%)	Women[b] (%)
No shock	68.0	24.7
Little or no time	10.0	16.9
Days	13.5	17.8
Weeks	6.5	21.9
1 year or more	2.0	11.4
Never	—	3.7

[a] Based on 215 experiences.
[b] Based on 531 experiences.
Source: Landis (1956).

Table 5.3. Reactions of confidants when told of child/adult sexual contact as recalled by adult interviewees, arranged in order of helpfulness[a]

	No.	%
Comfort and understanding	16	24
Play it down	6	9
Amusement (peer confidants only)	12	18
Curiosity (peer confidants only)	5	7
Anger with perpetrator	17	25
Shock	14	21
Forbid the child going to that place again	8	12
Ignored or didn't care	6	9
Disbelief	4	6
Anger with child	5	7
Total incidents confided in someone	67	100

[a] Individual reactions add up to more than the total number of incidents as some confidants reacted in more than one way.
Source: Nash and West (1985).

the character of many parents' responses. Nash and West add that 'police, social workers and GPs were often described as having failed to understand the child's feelings and to have made the situation worse' (p. 63).

The general point here is an important one: the effects of abuse are not just caused by the abuser and the abusive experience. Other adults, *well-intentioned or not*, also carry some responsibility for outcome, and it is not only parental reactions that can cause distress. Finkelhor (1986, p. 178) cautions against regarding long-term effects as the criterion for judging the seriousness of child sexual abuse. This view puts an even greater responsibility on those adults who deal with the child at the time of the incident.

LONG-TERM TRAUMA

Even when there appears to be no distress or trauma at the time, the child may need adult mediation to mitigate *future* psychological harm. In the study by Nash and West (1985) a significant minority of the women still considered themselves to be affected by their childhood abusive experience. And for all the women involved, the retrospective view of the incident was *never* positive even if the initial reaction had been. This suggests that the childhood experience has a 'sleeper' effect, so that even where a child appears to be psychologically unharmed, harm may emerge when the person views the experience from an adult perspective. In their retrospective reports of male and female college students, Fritz *et al.* (1981) actually found that those early experiences which were 'positive' caused the greatest distress for adult women. They comment:

> Positive as opposed to negative coercion appears to be
> correlated with self-perceived adult sexual
> maladjustment. The guilt induced by succumbing to
> molestation without physical force is the basic identified
> factor compounding the trauma associated with
> molestation such that its effect is felt in adult life.
> Conversely, the recipient of verbal threats or physical
> attack could absolve herself of culpability. (pp. 57–8)

It has to be said, however, that this inference does not seem to agree with the findings of the other investigators cited in this chapter, who are clear that the use of force by the abuser is a major factor associated with later reports of trauma and psychological disturbance.

Finkelhor (1979) gave extended consideration to those features of the abusive experience which were most traumatic to his subjects in their retrospective judgement. He identifies the following:

- the use of force (as mentioned above);
- abusers who are older adults;
- intrafamilial abuse;
- experiences as an older child. (He comments (p. 100), 'naivete may exert a protection against trauma,' i.e. greater awareness produces greater guilt; a similar point to that made by Fritz *et al.*, 1981.)

The supposed 'seriousness' of the act (on an adult scale from 'least contact' to 'most contact') was *not* related to trauma; nor was duration of abuse found to be significant. Brière and Runtz (1988), using somewhat different criteria (reporting levels of symptoms of psychological disturbance), found a remarkably similar pattern of association: older abusers, force and incest were related to reported disturbances, while 'seriousness' and duration of the abusive incidents were not related.

Baker and Duncan (1985) in their study of the prevalence of child sexual abuse in the UK conclude (p. 462): 'What is clear from this study is that the nature of the experience on its own does not determine the outcome and that other factors must be considered.' One major factor mediating outcome is the sex of the child: 'Overall males reported being significantly ($p = <0.001$) less damaged by their abusive experiences than women did.' A similar conclusion was reached by Goldman and Goldman (1988): 'girls ... appear to be at much greater risk of trauma in the long term.' They add, 'girls appear to be more traumatized by heterosexual experiences in the long term, while boys do not' (p. 101).

This brings in the issue of the effects of homosexual abusive experiences. By virtue of the fact that in the majority of studies abusers are shown mainly to be men, the experience of boys is much more likely to be homosexual. Finkelhor (1979, p. 103) concludes from his data that homosexuality was not the issue. 'The issue was whether the child's partner was a male or a female. Experiences with males were consistently more negative than experiences with females, whatever the sex of the child.... Boys' experiences with women were in general less traumatic than those with men.' Finkelhor's argument doesn't quite hold: his data show that homosexual experiences are *less* traumatic for girls and *more* traumatic for boys (for whom they usually constitute the majority).

It is a consistent finding that the outcomes of child sexual abuse are more serious for females; no study reports the reverse. And those studies which show the majority of abusers of boys to be female, also show the least negative outcome. Fritz *et al.* (1981) go so far as to assert that: 'Males are likely to view pre-pubescent contacts as sexual *initiation* while females view such encounters as sexual *violation*' (p. 59). This appears to be as true of the initial response as of the long-term retrospective evaluation of the experience. Why this should be requires explanation. It may have something to do with the differing sexual socialization of males and females in our society, where different standards of sexual experience are expected for girls and boys, women and men. Abused females are more likely to see themselves as 'damaged goods' in a way that abused males do not, this being a prime example of the way in which the effects of abusive incidents do not simply reside in the character of the incidents themselves.

Finkelhor and Browne (1986) propose four trauma-causing factors in the experience of sexual abuse (pp. 182–4):

1 *Traumatic sexualization*: 'in which a child's sexuality (including both sexual feelings and sexual attitudes) is shaped in a developmentally inappropriate and interpersonally dysfunctional fashion as a result of sexual abuse'.
2 *Betrayal*: 'in which children discover that someone on whom they are vitally dependent has caused them harm'.
3 *Powerlessness*: 'the process in which the child's will, desires, and sense of efficacy are continually contravened'.
4 *Stigmatization*: 'the negative connotations – for example, badness, shame and guilt – that are communicated to the child about the experiences and that then become incorporated into the child's self-image'.

Finkelhor's abstract scheme somehow underlines what we have to protect children against: the experiences themselves and the possible consequences for their psychological adjustment. It is not hard to see that sexual abuse could constitute a fundamental assault on the process of personality development. When children in the UK have to resort to calling 'Childline' to seek help (and even if we allow that some such calls are spurious), the strong implication is that the adults in many children's lives are *not* seen as a source of help. Prevention needs to be comprehensive and accessible. Chapters 6 and 7 develop this theme.

6
PREVENTION: CHILD-CENTRED APPROACHES

Since the early 1980s there has been a proliferation of prevention programmes using every conceivable medium: film, theatre, puppetry, books, comics, role-play, discussion groups, and so on. That prevention makes sense is not an issue; the problem is rather to demonstrate that it has been achieved, or even, which is more to the point, how it can be achieved.

Tharinger *et al.* (1988) comment: 'In the rush to respond to the prevalence of child sexual abuse it appears that many essential preliminary steps in the construction of prevention education programs have been ignored or skipped' (p. 615). And Repucci and Haugaard (1989) add what could be a footnote to this: 'having positive goals is not enough. Effectiveness of intervention is critical. Yet most programs appear to continue on the strength of their positive goals rather than on a systematic evaluation of their effectiveness' (p. 1268). These cautions will be at the heart of the review in this chapter. However, first we need to consider something of the background to the prevention movement, in particular why it has taken the form it has: primarily programmes targeted at children.

At an abstract level, Caplan's conceptual model of prevention in mental health (Caplan, 1964) has been widely employed. This encompasses primary, secondary and tertiary levels of prevention. In relation to child sexual abuse these can be described as:

- preventing abuse by eliminating causes or developing positive competence in children (*primary prevention*);
- identifying abuse sufficiently early for effective intervention to put a stop to it (*secondary prevention*);
- developing treatment programmes so as to reduce the possibility of future psychological impairment, i.e. to minimize the consequences of abuse (*tertiary prevention*).

Zax and Cowen (1976, p. 482) emphasize that 'tertiary prevention is prevention in name only'. Secondary prevention has also sometimes encompassed 'treatment' approaches at the family level, that is, to change the 'dynamics' of abuse and curtail it.

In a paper entitled 'Is treatment too late? What ten years of evaluative research tell us', Cohn and Daro (1987) review four major federally funded programmes in the USA which attempted to determine the relative effectiveness of different approaches to child abuse and neglect (including sexual abuse). They conclude:

> Treatment efforts in general are not very successful.... If
> research findings are to be of any use in setting policies,
> the results of a decade of evaluative research on
> treatment programs suggest that putting all resources
> into intervention after the fact does not make sense.
> (p. 440)

However, they do report that in one group of studies, improvements (in the abusive pattern of behaviour) were significantly better in families where sexual abuse was involved than in the more intractable area of child neglect. None the less, 'in every respect, the projects most successful in immediately eliminating abusive behavior were projects which generally separated the child from the abusive parent, either by placing the child in temporary foster care or requiring the maltreating parent to move out of the home' (p. 438).

Bearing in mind the known difficulty of changing behaviour, particularly in its more deviant forms, the professional enthusiasm for treatment via the 'talking' therapies is hard to understand. Bentovim *et al.* (1988), adherents of family therapy, reporting their findings in the UK, would seem to come to a conclusion (p. 266), similar to the above, that 'structural family change' rather than family 'treatment' is the main source of improvement.

Although there is a range of treatment programmes aimed at sexually abused children, an extensive literature search has failed to identify any that have been evaluated in a controlled fashion. General research on child psychotherapy (Levitt, 1957, 1971) reveals that improvement rates for 'untreated' children are the same as for 'treated' children. And Conte (1984), reviewing the professional response to sexually abused children, goes so far as to suggest that they may be subjected to 'therapy-induced trauma' as therapists continue to probe for feelings of victimization (p. 261).

Our main focus in this chapter will be on primary and secondary levels of intervention directed at children. Indirect approaches – aimed at potentially supportive adults – will be dealt with in Chapter 7. It has already been noted that direct-approach interventions are in the majority. We need to consider why that is so and why the young are, in effect, expected to protect themselves.

DIRECT-APPROACH PREVENTION PROGRAMMES

A widespread assumption is that it is children's lack of knowledge of sexual abuse, their social powerlessness and lack of relevant social skills which render them vulnerable. Finkelhor (1986) argues that the logic of direct approaches to intervention has emerged from clinical work with victims of sexual abuse which has indicated that they could have been spared vulnerability and suffering if they had had even very simple information about their right to refuse sexual advances or other inappropriate behaviour on the part of an adult. A similar case is made by Vernon and Hay (1988) to explain the rationale for a school implementation programme they developed:

> The need for such a program was felt by the second author, an elementary counselor, who was asked to counsel several children who had been sexually assaulted. In working with these children she was concerned about how to help them work through their traumatic experience and believed that if they had been aware of different kinds of touch, how to say no or the right to protect their bodies, they might not have been sexually abused. (pp. 306–7)

It is in response to such beliefs that programmes have been focused on children, with the implicit message (to all concerned) that sexual abuse is at least partly a function of their ignorance, lack of assertiveness and lack of power. Programmes vary considerably in the techniques of presentation employed, the target age of the child audience, the number of sessions involved and who actually presents the programme, whether 'specialist' or 'non-specialist'. However, there is greater consistency in content, and most programmes, for example, the best-known UK programme, 'Kidscape' (Elliott, 1985), include some or all of the following concepts:

body ownership: emphasizing that the child owns his or
her own body and controls access to it;
touching: (related to the above) the notion of, for
example, 'good' versus 'bad' touches;
saying 'no': the right to say 'no' when approached or
touched inappropriately;
escape: techniques of distancing and getting away from a
potential or possible abuser;
intuition: encouraging children to 'trust their own feelings'
if they feel that something is wrong;
secrets: the notion of appropriate versus inappropriate
secrets – aimed at foiling adult attempts to get children
'not to tell';
support persons: identifying adults whom children can
turn to for help, and encouraging them to do so.

Miller-Perrin and Wurtele (1988) comment:

> Intuitively, these concepts appear appropriate for
> teaching children self-protection, although it must be
> noted that presently we do not know the precise methods
> employed by perpetrators to engage and maintain
> children in sexual abuse situations, nor do we know what
> methods children actually employ to successfully escape
> from potential molestors. (p. 316)

The same point is made by Tharinger *et al.* (1988) who add: 'the
current set of concepts and skills taught in prevention programs are
based upon what adults believe will prevent sexual victimization'
(p. 619).

On the basis of these notions a large number of creative and enter-
taining programmes have been made – mainly in the US – some of
them to a highly professional level of production. But few have been
subjected to a controlled evaluation and, in any case, the process of
evaluation is itself problematic. Roberts *et al.* (1990) carried out a
questionnaire survey of 33 authors and publishers about the development of commercially available sexual abuse prevention materials.
Their results show that there had been little empirical validation of the
programmes during their development apart from 'informal field
testing'.

Repucci and Haugaard (1989) review those programmes which

have been subjected to some form of controlled evaluation; they are surprisingly few, and most studies display a number of shortcomings in their construction. In general, children who had been through training programmes did know more about the concepts covered at post-test but the increments were often very small (even when statistically significant) because the level of knowledge pre-test was often very high. This poses a question in itself: what is usefully being taught if children know most of the content anyway?

For example, a study by Binder and McNiel (1987), which pre- and post-tested children's knowledge of coping strategies in relation to potential abuse (but incorporated no control group), used a 13-item scale, each item being rated from 1 to 5, with 5 being the most knowledgeable. The results are shown in Table 6.1. The differences are

Table 6.1. Pre- and post-test mean scores obtained by children in the study by Binder and McNiel (1987)

	Pre-test mean	*Post-test mean*
Children aged 9–12 years	4.58	4.75
Children aged 5–8 years	4.63	4.75

statistically significant, but it is clear that the knowledge increment is tiny. Of course, the 'ceiling effects' shown here may be a function of an inadequate test instrument, i.e. too simple, too short and too obvious. Other researchers have reported similar problems, e.g. Wolfe *et al.* (1986). If the 'ceiling' of a test is too low, and the whole instrument is insufficiently sensitive, then knowledge gains will not be shown even if they are there. As Miller-Perrin and Wurtele (1988, p. 319) point out, 'In most studies, researchers have created and employed their own unique assessment devices that have face validity but that are of unknown reliability.'

These are technical, methodological problems that could conceivably be sorted out. But there are more fundamental problems with the 'knowledge-enhancement' approach. In the first place, programme concepts are often abstract, allusive or circumspect. Conte *et al.* (1985), in an evaluation of programme content with children aged 4 to 10 years, found that prevention concepts of an abstract, qualified nature, which required judgement and interpretation on the part of the child, presented much greater difficulty than concepts of a specific concrete nature. Repucci and Haugaard (1989) observe that 'young children are much better at following broad and general rules ... than they are at following rules that require making distinctions'. They add the interesting comment: 'Many adults have been in situations in which they know that something should be done, but, without a specific plan, they chose to do nothing rather than engage in a wrong or inefficient action' (p. 1267).

But whether vague or specific, programme content is likely to be ill-understood if children are not given some idea of what they have to protect themselves against. Notably there is an apparent reluctance on the part of programme authors to include content of a specifically sexual nature. There are probably several reasons for such an oblique approach. Miller-Perrin and Wurtele (1988) comment: 'It appears that many program developers have been willing to compromise on the explicitness of sexual information in order to have their program adopted by the school system' (p. 317). More charitable critics might say that the programme authors were concerned not to upset or frighten children; but the question of effectiveness remains.

Tharinger *et al.* (1988), reviewing 41 programmes commercially available in the USA, found that a minority of those directed at children used specific terms for genitalia: 'These data support the concern ... that sexual abuse prevention programs do not sufficiently provide labels for children and adolescents to use when communicating about sexual parts of their bodies' (p. 626). Other research by Sanford (1980) has emphasized that abused children may be inhibited in disclosure because they lack the vocabulary for, or experience in discussing, sex-related matters. Avoiding the use of anatomically 'correct' terms may put such children at risk.

A second weakness of the knowledge-enhancement approach is that most of these programmes teach (and test) changes in knowledge rather than changes in coping behaviours. This would not signify, of course, if changing behaviour were simply a matter of enabling children (or anybody else) to understand what they *ought* to do. Leventhal (1987) poses the problem succinctly:

> The ultimate goal of any program to prevent sexual abuse
> is to teach behaviours so that when an adult makes a
> sexual advance toward a child, the child will act in an
> appropriate manner by saying no and telling a
> responsible adult what happened. Yet none of the
> evaluative efforts has examined this direct outcome.

> Instead, a change in knowledge, which is really an
> intermediate measure, has been examined without any
> evidence that such a change is linked to changes in
> behavior. (p. 169)

A major problem in the treatment of adult chronically ill patients, who know *very clearly* the consequences of failing to comply with medical advice, is that they often fail to do so (e.g. in the case of hypertensive patients; Sackett *et al.*, 1975). If adults do not change their behaviour when the knowledge is specific and clear-cut, can it be assumed that knowledge, of vague application, will change children's behaviour in what may be a stressful and disturbing situation? Yet the equation of knowledge with behaviour is often tacitly assumed in the literature. For example, Swan, Press and Briggs (1985), in an evaluation of a sexual abuse prevention programme (a play followed by a discussion) with 63 children aged 8 to 11 years, found that significantly more children at post-test selected the response 'tell someone' if they should experience a sexual assault. The authors conclude (p. 402) that 'the play and following discussion did teach the children to report sexual assault'. Nothing of the sort: it taught them that they *ought to report* sexual assault.

Obviously children cannot be exposed to abusive situations, real or simulated, in the name of research. But, at the same time, the status of inadequately evaluated programmes is in itself a matter of professional ethical concern. Repucci and Haugaard (1989) put it bluntly: 'There is no evidence, not even one published case example, that primary prevention has ever been achieved. Often it is assumed that these programs work because well-meaning professionals and parents believe that they do' (p. 1274).

What can be done about this dilemma? Four complementary approaches present themselves, and there is some evidence to support each. First, we can incorporate *role-play techniques* into preventive programmes, i.e. actually training children in appropriate behaviours in enacted situations: what is usually known as 'participant modelling'. Second, we can construct *simulated encounters* with 'strangers' (for ethical reasons, without a sexual or physically coercive component). Third, we can ascertain whether following a programme intervention, children spontaneously report past or present experiences of sexual abuse, so that the programme itself appears *to facilitate disclosure*. Fourth, we can investigate the actual *techniques employed by child molesters*, when children are at their most vulnerable, and the *self-protective strategies* children have themselves employed to cope with these advances.

ROLE-PLAY TECHNIQUES

The social learning theorist, Albert Bandura, claimed that treatments involving actual performance produced results consistently superior to those based on 'symbolic' forms of instruction (Bandura, 1977). *Participant modelling* (PM) involves actively practising a skill whereas *symbolic modelling* (SM) involves watching others perform the skill (live or on film). The former is thought to increase the probability that an individual will be able to perform the skill when necessary. There is some empirical support for this claim (see review by Klingman *et al.*, 1984).

However, research by Wurtele *et al.* (1986, 1987) provides only very limited support for the superiority of PM over SM, as reflected in improvements on two test measures of knowledge about personal safety and coping with hypothetical abusive situations. In the 1986 study, children of average age 6 years and average age 11 years were divided into four groups. Some were given a behavioural skills training programme (PM); others watched a film covering similar content (SM); a third group was given both forms of training (PM and SM); and a control group had both forms of training but *after* the post-test (and for whom follow-up scores were not available).

Immediate post-testing showed significant differences on one of the test variables (personal safety) for those who had received the participant modelling part of the training programme. But at the three-month follow-up the scores of the 'film only' children had increased to a level comparable with the other treatment groups. Furthermore differences between *all* groups (including the control) at any time were extremely small: less than 2 points on the 13-point personal safety questionnaire and less than 4 points on the 32-point 'what if' situations test.

The 1987 study involved 26 5-year-old children, the same test measures, and equal length 'live' PM and SM training sessions. Both groups were post-tested following their first sessions. The SM group then received the PM programme and both groups were tested again. On both post-tests the original PM group did significantly better on the 'what if' situations test – although the difference was smaller at the second post-test. After six weeks the follow-up showed there was no difference between the groups, although differences were at no point very large.

The results, overall, are therefore neither very strong nor very illuminating. But again the outcome measured was changes in *knowledge*. It may be that if the outcome measure had involved performance, a more significant effect might have been demonstrated for PM.

SIMULATED ENCOUNTERS

An investigation which addressed the problem presented by this difficult evaluation criterion was that of Fryer *et al.* (1987a, 1987b). The investigation did not use a specific sexual abuse prevention programme but via role-play taught children definite rules to follow if they were approached by a stranger when they were not with a caretaking adult. Children aged 6 to 8 years were involved, 23 in the experimental group and 21 in the control group (who were given the role-play activities later). The day before and after the training 'programme' each child was sent on an errand by his or her teacher, and met a male member of the research team (unknown to the child) who asked the child to come to his car to bring something into the school. Great care was taken by the researchers to inform parents and to monitor children's reactions for possible signs of distress.

At pre-test about half the children agreed to go with the 'stranger'. But at post-test only 22 per cent of the 'programme' group did so, although there was no change in the control group.

After a six-month interval, 'programme' children who had failed the post-test and children in the control group were given the role-play training. Then all the children (including those 'programme' children who were successful on the original post-test) were again given the 'real-life' test. All of the children from both groups passed the test this time except for two of the retrained children.

These are impressive results, but a few comments are necessary. First, the training was very specific (i.e. dealing with approaches from strangers) to the test situation. Second, the rules taught were concrete and did not require much interpretation (see the previous discussion on this point). Third, the 'testing' itself could be construed as part of the training experience. Finally, the fact that two children still failed the test situation gives some indication of individual children's vulnerability. However, Repucci and Haugaard (1989) comment: 'Such assessments represent the best means of estimating the strength of the behaviors and should be pursued whenever appropriate' (p. 1272).

THE FACILITATION OF DISCLOSURE

As already noted, one of the major components of sexual abuse/ stranger abduction prevention programmes is that children are encouraged to tell a trusted adult if they are approached in this way. One form of evaluation, therefore, would be to see if disclosure rates increase after a programme presentation. This has not been investigated systematically although there are a number of incidental reports of such disclosures, gathered at little more than anecdotal level. For example, Garbarino (1987) in a simple individual interview follow-up of children who had read a special edition of *Spiderman* comic (dealing with methods of self-help in relation to sexual abuse) reported that

> one boy produced a 20-minute exposition on the comic's strengths and weaknesses. Finally, he turned and said, 'This is just what happened to me.' And he proceeded to tell of being sexually molested by a teenage neighbor over a period of a year and a half starting when he was in second grade. He was silent over that period to protect his mother from the harm the neighbor threatened to inflict upon her if he told. The boy concluded, 'He said he would put soap suds in her eyes and put her in the washing machine and he has a black belt in karate and he said he would get her.' Finally the boy was asked if having had the *Spiderman* comic at the time the molestation began would have made a difference. 'Yes,' he replied, 'I would have told my mom about it. I wouldn't have been so afraid. I would have known it was right to tell.' (p. 148)

Conte *et al.* (1985) make the point that 'programs which have been presented to children and have failed to identify any abused children either during training, or shortly thereafter, appear to be doing something wrong in view of the fact that somewhere around 20 per cent of the girls and 10 per cent of the boys will be abused before they reach 18' (p. 328).

Leventhal (1987) carries the research implications a little further:

> one approach might be to conduct a survey after an intervention program has been given to a group of children to determine whether any child during the subsequent three to six months has told an adult about another adult's inappropriate behaviour toward him or

her. Such a survey might be conducted by interviewing an adult in the family, such as the mother. An identical survey also could be conducted in a control population. If the survey was conducted 'blindly' and there were more reports of children in the intervention group who told adults, then such findings would provide support for the belief that the teaching programme was effective.

Although the prevalence of sexual abuse is high, before conducting such a trial it would be important to calculate the size of sample necessary to detach a statistically significant difference in the rates of telling between the groups, especially since little is known about how often children in a general population say no and do tell a responsible adult. (p. 170)

It is surprising that there is such a paucity of research on this important point. What evidence there is has not been published in conventional form. For example, Kent (1979) found that one-sixth of the children attending a particular classroom presentation subsequently revealed a prior sexual assault; of these, one-half had never reported the incident before. And Beland (1985) reported that the disclosure rate in schools taking part in prevention programmes was 'significantly higher' compared with schools not participating. Hazzard *et al.* (1988) reported that out of 286 8- and 9-year-old children who had gone through a school-based sexual abuse prevention programme, eight children subsequently disclosed ongoing abuse, and 20 others told about past occurrences. However, the authors did not go on to assess the validity of these revelations and simply comment that 'although follow-up information was not available on all disclosures, we were not made aware of any disclosures which were subsequently felt to be false allegations by school personnel or Protective Services' (p. 19).

Of course, this sort of outcome has to be seen as evidence of secondary prevention rather than primary prevention, but its importance is not diminished by that, and the need for further, systematic research is clearly indicated.

INVESTIGATING STRATEGIES USED BY CHILD MOLESTERS AND IDENTIFYING VULNERABLE BEHAVIOUR

Because this is an area where specific research data are lacking, it follows that prevention programmes are based, at best, on general features of the sexual abuse research data, combined with clinical anecdote. It is likely that many programmes could not even claim that much basis for their content. The amount of overlap between programmes suggests a form of plagiarism, the recycling of untested assumptions – in particular, the assumption that we know the kinds of skills which will make a child less vulnerable to sexual attack.

Some data bearing on this issue are reported by Showers *et al.* (1983) and Farber *et al.* (1984), focusing mainly on the forms of coercion, verbal and physical, reported by child sexual abuse victims. Budin and Johnson (1989) comment:

> Studies involving victims of sexual abuse have
> shortcomings. The ages of victims and the emotional
> stress that they have undergone may preclude their
> ability to recall the details of their exploitation. *Moreover,
> it is unlikely that younger children are able to fully
> comprehend the consequences or extent of their
> manipulation.* (p. 78; emphasis added)

This last point could be overcome to some extent by asking young adults to report and evaluate retrospectively incidents in their childhood, but as we have seen there are problems attendant on that kind of attempt to reassess past experiences.

To get over this problem, Budin and Johnson (1989) decided to approach from the other side. They used adult reports, but concentrated their investigation on the perpetrators. They asked 72 male prisoners, who had convictions for sexual offences against children, to provide information about how and where they found their victims, and how they gained or enforced their co-operation. They were also asked to indicate what they thought children should be taught to prevent their own sexual abuse. Their 'recommendations' are summarized in Figure 6.1. It should be noted that approximately half the offenders reported that their victims were related to them, but this does *not* mean that half of the victims were related to their abuser. Individual offenders reported that they had abused up to *200* children.

The overall findings, as Budin and Johnson observe, 'indicate that

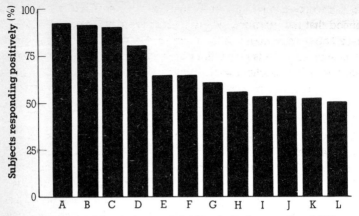

Figure 6.1. Recommendations by incarcerated child molesters for prevention of child sexual abuse. The subjects were asked which of the following they believed should be taught to children so that they could prevent their own sexual abuse:

A tell if they have been abused
B say 'no'
C learn about proper touching of their privates by others
D never get into a stranger's car
E run away if approached
F resist
G keep away from strangers
H cry
I have better parents
J do not talk to strangers
K never tell one's name
L shout if an adult approaches (from Budin and Johnson, 1989).

aspects of current prevention programs may be efficacious' (p. 84). A complementary, but clearly indicated, research need is for children's reports (whether current or retrospective) as to how they *effectively* dealt with potential abusers. Successful strategies that children *actually* use are more likely to be employed than adult inventions. Accurate programme content is, of course, no guarantee of effective self-protection, but it has a greater chance of success than inaccurate or wrongly presented or focused content.

REACTIONS TO PROGRAMME PRESENTATION

This chapter has dealt with prevention approaches to sexual abuse that directly focus on the child. Whether effective or not, such a direct emphasis presents its own problems. In the first place, it could be claimed that the programmes themselves are disturbing to children; for example, they might cause them to distrust all adults. To some extent such arguments may reflect adult embarrassment or feelings of inadequacy in broaching sexual topics with children. This is not to argue that programme developers should not be alive to the possibility of unintended negative side-effects, particularly when dealing with very young children.

A number of empirical studies have addressed the issue, at one level or another. Kleemeier and Webb (1986) – cited in Repucci and Haugaard, 1989 – used a parental questionnaire in a controlled study and reported that 35 per cent of the children displayed negative emotional reactions and 20 per cent exhibited negative behavioural reactions. Garbarino (1987) in a follow-up of children who had read the special edition of *Spiderman* comic found that when interviewed, and in response to a direct question, between 17 and 50 per cent of the children (at different age levels and of different sexes) replied that they were worried or 'scared' afterwards.

Other studies have reported much lower, even negligible, negative reactions. Miller-Perrin and Wurtele (1988) found that 11 per cent of the parents of 12-year-olds who had watched a sexual abuse prevention film or taken part in a behavioural skills training programme, reported negative effects. Swan *et al.* (1985) evaluated children's and parents' reactions to a play presentation, the children being aged 8 to 11 years; 7 per cent of the parents reported that their children did not like the play, 5 per cent that their children were upset, but none that their child felt negative about attending the play.

Binder and McNiel (1987) evaluated a school-based programme involving separate workshops for children aged 5 to 12 years, and parents and teachers. After the programme both children and adults overwhelmingly reported feeling safer and more confident; only 3 per cent reported feeling more 'scared'.

Nibert *et al.* (1989) address the question of whether very young children (4 to 5 years) with their more limited understanding might be more disturbed through misunderstanding and the inability to refine concepts. Working in seven Head Start Centers in Columbus, Ohio, they presented three 20-minute workshops over three days followed by informal discussion between presenters and children. Some 650 questionnaires were sent home to parents asking for details of their children's reactions to the programme and also to what degree they talked to their children about sexual abuse. Of the 34 per cent of the questionnaires returned 26 per cent of the respondents reported a positive response to the programme, 7.2 per cent reported a negative or problematic response, while 65.9 per cent observed no significant behavioural change. Interestingly, 64 per cent of the parents also said that they had discussed the topic of sexual abuse with their children before the programme. The authors conclude with an emphasis that prevention approaches should aim to *empower* children rather than frighten them.

The notion of 'empowerment' is an intuitively attractive one. For example, Butler (1986) argues:

> Programs that teach prevention within the framework of empowerment are premised on the belief that one primary reason children are abused and molested is because they are powerless. Children are potential victims because they are small, vulnerable, without many resources, and with insufficient information or skills to protect themselves. (p. 8)

There is, however, a gradient between giving individuals more self-assertive and self-protective power and making them responsible for their self-defence. Wurtele (1987) marks the line of responsibility: 'Children should not be made responsible for protecting themselves or to feel guilty when they do not respond appropriately' (p. 487). Self-protection has to be part of a network of protective support for children.

We have seen earlier that children who have experienced a sexual abuse prevention programme appear to be more likely to disclose previous or current abuse. Presumably the programme content – and the fact that it is presented by authoritative adults – confers a kind of social permission on disclosure and enables the child to tell someone. It is likely that the programmes also provide a *language of disclosure*: a 'respectable' vocabulary for talking about sexual acts and body parts and a clear sanction that it is acceptable to do so.

It may be that there is a similar effect on the child's behaviour in potentially abusive situations. We have seen that children usually know much of what they *should* do before they are given the 'prevention' programmes, but experience of the programme may 'organize' the knowledge better for use and provide *adult authority* to support a child when faced with the approaches of a 'powerful' adult abuser.

However, a shift in power and authority relationships has several elements and comes from several directions. In Chapter 7 we shall consider the various *indirect* ways in which child sexual abuse may be prevented.

7

PROTECTING CHILDREN FROM SEXUAL ABUSE

In what could be regarded as a footnote to Chapter 6, Swift (1979) gives us the direction for the present one:

> Conventionally the prevention of sexual assault has focussed on altering the behavior of the victim. Through self-defense training, proscriptions of behavior resulting in vulnerability to attack (don't accept rides from strangers, don't go out alone at night, don't walk through parks alone, etc.) women and children are cautioned to make themselves less accessible to sexual assault. The result of these measures is not the prevention of sexual assault, but the prevention of sexual assault of cautious women and children, and those proficient in the physical martial arts. The attacker continues to victimize the young, the weak, the vulnerable or the uninformed. Sexual assault is not prevented by this approach, but rather displaced. (p. 133)

It is not the purpose of the present chapter to turn the previous one on its head, to suggest that the child-centred prevention movement is entirely misguided, although the almost total lack of any adequate evaluation of these prevention programmes must be taken very seriously. They have to be seen as part (and perhaps only a small part) of a more comprehensive approach to protecting children from sexual abuse and its consequences.

On the evidence, child-centred programmes are likely to be most necessary, and most effective, in helping children to deal with approaches from *strangers* because, first, this is the category of abusers that caretaking adults are least able to protect children from; and because, second, the rules for dealing with strangers are simpler and require less interpretation (don't enter into conversation, don't get too close, get away as soon as possible) and so are more workable (Repucci and Haugaard,1989; Fryer *et al.*, 1987a, 1987b). It is for these reasons that the prevention programmes developed by the author have focused on the threat posed by 'deviant' strangers (Gillham, 1988, 1989). Although, as we have seen in Chapter 2, it is *not* the largest problem, it is more likely to include the most serious forms of abuse and assault.

Expecting children to protect themselves from people they *know* is quite another matter. Children are, on the whole, remarkably compliant: they trust easily (and who would want them to be fearful, mistrustful and suspicious?). Any adult going into a situation (school or family) where there are young children, and where the adult is accepted by the adult caretakers, is rapidly accepted as a 'friend' by the children. Yet it is this 'known' category of implicitly trusted (or at least unsuspected) adults which often constitutes the largest category of risk. From the evidence we have reviewed in Chapter 2 it would seem that caretakers make a poor job of protecting their children in this respect, and are insufficiently cautious on their behalf. There are two questions we need to consider in detail: 'Who is it that caretakers (whether parents or teachers) have to protect children against?' and 'What can we do about the perpetrators themselves?'

WHO ARE THE PERPETRATORS?

This is a topic redolent with mythology: active myths that disarm protecting adults and provide a form of cover for those who *actually* molest children.

Although the data on the relationship of abuser to victim have been considered, we have not yet given an indication of the typical age of the child abuser. Whilst it may be recognized that the notion of the child molester as a furtive old man in a raincoat is an exaggerated stereotype, it is not generally appreciated that abusers are commonly young – in their late teens, twenties and early thirties – and sexually active in a general sense. It is also a consistent finding that the abusers of boys are significantly younger than the abusers of girls. Finkelhor (1979) gives an average estimated age for abusers of boys as 26.9 years, as against 31.7 years for abusers of girls. Goldman and Goldman (1988), in their methodologically similar Australian study, give average estimated ages of 22.4 years and 30.5 years respectively. Nash and West (1985), in their study of two groups of females, give an estimated average age of 35 years for the abuser.

These data can be presented in a different way to emphasize the point that is being made (Table 7.1). Three prevalence studies give percentages of abusers aged under 30 and over 50 for both male and female victims. It will be recalled from Chapter 2 that boys are abused, on average, at an older age than girls so that the age difference between victim and abuser is generally much greater for girls than boys; and we know that this is associated with greater trauma.

Although there are undoubtedly pathological, persistent child molesters (see later), who do represent a real and disproportionate hazard to the child population, it is clear from the age and prevalence data in general that adult sexual involvement with children is, to some extent, a function or manifestation of the peak level of sexual activity, particularly in males (Kinsey *et al.*, 1948). It would be a mistake to assume that the potential abuser is going to appear 'odd' or 'peculiar'.

The 'individual pathology' model of the child molester has long been the common-sense view and has received some support from clinical studies and studies of incarcerated offenders, e.g. Erickson *et al.* (1988). But such groups may not be typical of sexual abusers as a whole. The age data we have presented, and the relatively wide-spread nature of the problem, lead to the conclusion that, *for a proportion of men at least, abuse is probably characteristic of their sexual behaviour.*

Without being chronically suspicious or paranoid, parents need to consider why *any* adult seeks to involve himself with their children, especially if the relationship is one which lends itself to opportunities for sexual abuse. A similar reservation has to be applied to those who take up professional or voluntary roles which put them into positions of authority over children – an easily exploited situation. Whatever the personal characteristics of child abusers might be, *accessibility* to children is a major factor: hence the greater risk of abuse by step-fathers and other father-substitutes, that is, men who do not feel constrained by the incest taboo and find themselves (or put themselves) in a situation where sexual access is possible. The cynic who observed that sex is 5 per cent motivation and 95 per cent opportunity might, in some circumstances at least, have had child sexual abuse in mind.

If we are to protect our children, and since sexual abuse is more common than we may have realized, then it makes sense for us to exercise caution on their behalf, and to take direct action where necessary. Any adult who seeks to be on his own with a child, or in situations where the child is undressing or bathing or going to bed, needs to be 'checked out' in some way. A significant proportion of

Table 7.1. Percentages of abusers with estimated ages under 30 and over 50 for male and female victims

Study	Male victims		Female victims	
	Abusers under 30 (%)	Abusers over 50 (%)	Abusers under 30 (%)	Abusers over 50 (%)
Landis (1956)	51	3	39.6	9.8
Finkelhor (1979)	60.9	0[a]	57.1	7.6[a]
Goldman and Goldman (1988)	77.5	2.5	44.7	12.8

[a] aged 50 and over.

offences, for example, is committed by babysitters. The perpetrator's home is another 'risky' context (Wyatt, 1985).

Parents cannot, of course, protect their children from themselves. Guidance offered to teachers and others on the supposed 'diagnostic' signs of child sexual abuse is, as we have seen in Chapter 4, heavily flawed and likely to be unreliable. However, schools can create an atmosphere where the topic of sexual abuse is aired and acknowledged, so that children feel permitted to talk about their doubts or concerns in this respect. Children in well-known risk categories, for example, girls not living with their natural father, could be given an extra element of surveillance and personal attention which might make disclosure easier where an abusive relationship is developing.

WHY SHOULD ANYONE WANT TO ABUSE CHILDREN?

Many adults *could* abuse children: they have ample opportunity and the trust of their charges. But such a thing never crosses their minds. We need to go back to the fundamental question: what is it about those adults who take such opportunities or actively seek to create them? What makes them like that?

'Child sexual abuse' is an umbrella term covering a wide range of behaviour in many different settings. There can be no single explanation. In particular the persistent offender is likely to be in a quite different category from someone who commits a single offence under exceptional circumstances.

Araji and Finkelhor (1986), reviewing the literature, suggest that theories fall into four groups (p. 92) which seek to explain:

1 why a person would find relating sexually to a child to be emotionally gratifying and congruent (in the sense of the child fitting the adult's needs);

2 why a person would be capable of being sexually aroused by a child;

3 why a person would be frustrated or blocked in efforts to obtain sexual and emotional gratification from more normatively approved sources;

4 why a person would not be deterred by the conventional social restraints and inhibitions against having sexual relations with a child.

These four 'explanatory' factors can be summarized as *emotional congruence*, *sexual arousal*, *blockage* and *disinhibition*. They are not so much competing terms as complementary ones.

The main notion behind emotional congruence is that the child molesters are 'immature' or low in self-esteem and so feel more mature and sure of themselves in relation to young children (it should be recalled that it is pre-pubertal children who are most at risk). It is not at all clear why some adults are sexually aroused by children: most explanatory assumptions are unverified or unverifiable. They include such theories as early sexual experiences in childhood (with other children) being more satisfactory than adult sexual experiences, and the availability of child pornography (which may well *maintain* such an orientation even if it doesn't cause it).

Blockage theories can be seen as the obverse of emotional congruence theories, i.e. they presume that child molesters are 'blocked' in their ability to derive sexual and emotional satisfaction in adult heterosexual relationships. This is likely to be part of wider difficulties in relating to other adults, and perhaps to repressive sexual norms which make adult sexual relationships a matter of guilt and anxiety.

The idea of disinhibition is perhaps the most powerful explanation. It moves away from the 'personal pathology' emphasis of the other three theory groups into one where individual dispositions interact with situational opportunities and the wider context of social and cultural factors. For example, such a perspective would go a long way towards explaining why some men feel it is 'all right' to make sexual advances towards their step-daughters. And alcohol (a widely recognized 'disinhibitor') has often been implicated in incidents of child sexual abuse (e.g. Rada, 1976).

WERE CHILD MOLESTERS THEMSELVES VICTIMS OF ABUSE?

Simple, single-factor explanations of complex problems are extremely attractive. In the area of child sexual abuse it is the idea that molesters had themselves been abused in childhood. Such notions have been taken up by journalists and promoted by some professionals, e.g. the paper by Blanchard (1987), entitled 'Male victims of child sexual abuse: a portent of things to come'.

Blanchard cites a study by Groth (1979) in which he reports that 45 per cent of rapists were sexually assaulted as children. In another study of convicted offenders, Groth *et al.* (1978) found that 33 per cent had been sexually assaulted in childhood. These rates are high (two or three times the rates for males in prevalence studies) but a similar caution operates as was invoked in considering the effects of child sexual abuse in Chapter 5: because events in the past co-vary with events in the present, that does not necessarily mean that one *causes* the other.

For example, in a study of 229 convicted child molesters, Erickson *et al.* (1988) report that 86 per cent of offenders described themselves as homosexual or bisexual: a very high percentage. But this does *not* mean that being homosexual or bisexual 'causes' men to sexually abuse boys – nor does it 'explain' the abuse. Convicted child molesters are a special group – so flagrant and persistent that they are caught and convicted – a pathological sub-group. They probably also come from disadvantaged sectors of the community, with other 'causes' for their behaviour. It does not follow that their life history is representative of child molesters as a whole.

WHY IS IT MAINLY MEN WHO MOLEST CHILDREN?

If being sexually abused as a child led one to become an abuser then women, who are most often abused in childhood, would constitute the majority of abusers and, in most studies, they do not. Writers such as Blanchard (1987) suggest that males and females deal with emotional trauma differently, arguing that:

> Emotional repression, as an effort to preserve one's
> masculine image, greatly limits a man in overcoming the
> sexual traumas of his past. Furthermore, if anger,
> intimacy and sex become intertwined as a result of his
> refusal to deal with his full range of emotions, serious
> problems can develop. At best he may experience a
> series of conflictual relationships; at worst he may rape.
> (pp. 22–3)

However, as we have seen in Chapter 5, men report far fewer, and far less severe, negative reactions to their abusive experiences than women, this finding being consistent across several studies. Presumably Blanchard would argue that men are 'repressing' their trauma. But this is the familiar psychodynamic catch-all which explains everything and nothing.

A different perspective is to consider what it is about female psychology that makes them less likely than men to abuse children. It would seem that the sexual socialization of women may include elements which make them more responsible in sexual and other relationships. The issue is given extended consideration by Finkelhor (1986, p. 126 *et seq.*) and is briefly summarized here:

- women are less concerned to be dominant/assertive in sexual relationships;
- they are less disposed to have casual or multiple sexual relationships or to treat sex in isolation;
- they better distinguish non-sexual from sexual affection;
- they are less affected in terms of self-esteem by the unavailability of sexual opportunities;
- they are more sensitive to the care needs of children;
- sexual contact with children may be more prohibited by the female subculture;
- women may be able to empathize more with those who are abused.

THE PERSISTENT CHILD MOLESTER

Because it is now recognized that the frequency of sexual relationships with children is much more widespread amongst the male subculture than previously acknowledged, that does not mean that there is not a pathological sub-group of child molesters, atypical in their history and pattern of behaviour. Indeed, we have cautioned above about generalizing from this group to child molesters as a whole.

Most men who molest children do so when they are relatively young and sexually at their most active. The persistent offender is a different case, as is shown by those small number of studies which have looked at recidivism rates over a long period of time. Such studies, by their very nature, are rare but extremely important as a strand in prevention in relation to penal policy. Most studies follow up offenders for only a comparatively short period: three to five years. The number of studies which have carried out very long-term follow-ups is extremely small.

The Danish study of Christiansen *et al.* (1965) – cited in Soothill and Gibbens, 1978 – followed up 2,934 sex offenders over periods of 12 to 24 years, during which time 24.3 per cent were reconvicted, rather less than half (10 per cent) for sexual offences, although the likelihood of recidivism to the same type of sexual offence was greatest in the most deviant forms of sexual crime, i.e. involving children.

Soothill and Gibbens argue that the Danish study underestimates 'true' recidivism because it fails to take into account differential periods 'at risk', i.e. when offenders were imprisoned and so not out in the community, or deceased, or where the period of follow-up observation was less than the maximum. Their own study, although smaller (184 offenders) is particularly suited to the theme of this book because they identified those who had committed the offences of rape, incest and unlawful sexual intercourse with girls under 13: by any definition the most serious forms of child sexual abuse. The group they studied was made up of all those charged with at least one of these offences and appearing in the higher courts of England and Wales during 1951 and 1961, except for those acquitted or whose files could not be located.

Recalculating their data to allow for differential periods at risk, Soothill and Gibbens arrive at some disturbing conclusions. They argue that their data suggest:

> ... there is something special about the recidivism rates
> of these sexual offenders. We could estimate that about
> half of this sample of serious offenders against young
> girls would be re-convicted by the end of a follow-up
> period of 23 years (many of these will be ordinary
> property offenders whose sexual offence was quite
> atypical). About one-quarter of the sample will be re-

convicted of a sexual or violence offence (usually a rather serious one); many of these re-convictions will be after the men have spent a considerable time at freedom. *The important question is the nature of the supposedly crime-free period before their subsequent conviction for a sex or violence offence.* Elsewhere (Soothill, Jack and Gibbens, 1976) we have said that 'one might suggest that the unduly aggressive individual or the sexually maladjusted have a long-lasting "Achilles heel" normally held in check by compensatory satisfactions of pressures but liable to re-emerge in times of stress. This would certainly agree with clinical experience of discussing life histories of crime. *But it may be that [they] committed offences which often go unreported or undetected, so that chance factors play a large part.*' (p. 275; emphasis added)

We know that only a small proportion of sexual offences are even reported to the police, let alone come to court or result in a conviction. The high re-conviction rate for serious sexual crimes against girls in this study (which parallels the same authors' study of rapists (Soothill, Jack and Gibbens, 1976) referred to in the quotation above) almost certainly masks a much higher rate of re-offending by these groups of men – some of whom probably commit multiple offences. The implication is clear: the serious sex offender is also likely to be the *persistent* sex offender.

DO ADULTS DO ENOUGH TO PROTECT CHILDREN?

Earlier the need was indicated for parents (and others) to 'check out' adults who, formally or informally, are involved with their children and to note anything suspicious. Unfortunately, we find that suspicions are rarely acted on. Indeed, even when children report abusive incidents to their parents (Gagnon, 1965; Nash and West, 1985) no action is usually taken. There may well be an understandable mixture of reasons for this, but uncertainty about what constitutes appropriate or desirable action and an overlay of social embarrassment appear to predominate. It is not just children who fail to report, but adults also on their behalf; the persistent child molester is, in effect, shielded by this reluctance or uncertainty. Even when there are multiple indicators that an abusive situation is developing, there may be no effective action. Voicing such suspicions is not an easy matter, especially when there is no clear 'proof'.

A good example of this irresolution is provided by Sloan (1989). In February 1986 a primary school headteacher in Cornwall was suspended and later charged with indecent assault against three pupils and given a custodial sentence. It emerged that abuse had been going on over a ten-year period, that there had been many indications of possible abuse, though none definitive in themselves, and that a number of people had been suspicious. Sloan comments (p. 13): 'neither parents nor professionals had a clear notion of the action to take should they suspect a colleague of abuse.'

Whether suspected individuals are prosecuted or not, bringing the possibility of sexual abuse out into the open often leads to protective action. MacMurray (1989) refers to this as 'informal justice': evidence may not be legally adequate but the suspected abuser is 'warned off' and other adults can move to protect the child. The failure to air suspicions that have some foundation accords the possible abuser immunity.

SUMMARY CONCLUSIONS AND RECOMMENDATIONS

The orientation of this book has been towards establishing a sound basis for prevention: hence the emphasis on *evidence* and its evaluation.

Having presented the facts about child sexual abuse, we can best summarize what is likely to be effective, and what needs to be done, under the three headings of: *primary* prevention (stopping it from happening in the first place); *secondary* prevention (intervening in an abusive situation); and *tertiary* prevention (minimizing the adverse psychological effects of abuse).

Primary prevention

1 Increasing awareness of parents, teachers and other caretakers that child molesters are to be found at all levels of society, are often young or youngish men (and sometimes women) who may be in positions of

    responsibility towards children or may seek other involvement with children.

2 Recognizing that boys are almost as much at risk as girls, *particularly after the age of 10.*

3 Teaching children simple rules about dealing with approaches from strangers (because caretaker help may not be available, because rule interpretation is simpler, and because the only adequate evidence for effectiveness is in this category (Fryer *et al.*, 1987a, 1987b).

4 Teaching children *specific* information about access to private/sexual parts of their body – again because rules can be made relatively simple.

5 Establishing a more conspicuous social vigilance about child sexual abuse so that potential abusers might be deterred.

6 Establishing a penal policy which removes from circulation serious and persistent child molesters because they represent a disproportionate and long-term risk to the child population.

7 Providing children with education in personal–social relationships so as to sensitize them to interpersonal abuse in all forms.

Secondary prevention

1 Creating an atmosphere in schools and families (by formal and informal means) whereby children feel able to report abuse; and providing them with a vocabulary – at least for body parts – which will enable and permit them to disclose abuse they are experiencing.

2 Parents, teachers and others *acting* on their suspicions (which may result in *primary* prevention, if a persistent abuser is stopped).

3 Teachers, in particular, being alert to signs of sexual abuse in children (principally oblique forms of disclosure) but *not* relying on supposed behavioural or psychological indicators, most of which are non-specific to any aetiology, let alone sexual abuse.

4 A clear recognition of the fact that children rarely lie about sexual abuse.

5 Vigilance in the case of 'at risk' children, especially girls who are not with their natural fathers (an increasingly large category because of current rates of divorce and separation).

6 When the offender is in the child's home *removing him* or, if that is impossible, removing the child.

Tertiary prevention

1 Providing a sympathetic, undramatic, supportive response to the disclosure.

2 Keeping formal interviewing and 'treatment' to a minimally intrusive level.

3 Communicating to children that blame and responsibility are not theirs even if they 'co-operated' or 'consented'.

4 Providing counselling services for adults who have current adjustment problems attributable to sexual abuse in childhood.

POSTSCRIPT

Topics of social concern have their fashions: child sexual abuse has been 'fashionable' in the 1980s. If it becomes less so in the current decade that may be no bad thing, because some of the professional practice has been hasty and ill-conceived, and some of the published material which has been generated has been superficial and sensationalist. But serious study of the subject confirms its importance. And there are important implications that come from it, not least that child sexual abuse appears to be part of a wider problem of sexual abuse in our sort of society, a subject that warrants further study and may require social changes way beyond the scope of the recommendations outlined above.

REFERENCES

Asterisked (*) references are recommended for reading in the original.

Araji, S. and Finkelhor, D. (1986) Abusers: A review of research. In D. Finkelhor (ed.), *A Sourcebook on Child Sexual Abuse*. Beverly Hills, CA: Sage Publications.

Ariès, P. (1962) *Centuries of Childhood*. London: Jonathan Cape.

Armstrong, L. (1978) *Kiss Daddy Goodnight*. New York: Hawthorn.

Bagley, C. (1990) Is the prevalence of child sexual abuse decreasing? Evidence from a random sample of 750 young adult women. *Psychological Reports*, **66**(3), 1037–8.

*****Baker, A. W. and Duncan, S. P.** (1985) Child sexual abuse: A study of prevalence in Great Britain. *Child Abuse and Neglect*, **9**(4), 457–67.

Bandura, A. (1977) *Social Learning Theory*. Englewood Cliffs, NJ: Prentice-Hall.

Beland, K. (1985) *Prevention of Child Sexual Victimization: A School-based Statewide Prevention Model* (summary report). Seattle: Committee for Children.

Bentovim, A., Elton, A., Hildebrand, J., Tranter, M. and Vizard, E. (eds) (1988) *Child Sexual Abuse within the Family*. London: John Wright.

Binder, R. L. and McNiel, D. E. (1987) Evaluation of a school-based sexual abuse prevention program: Cognitive and emotional effects. *Child Abuse and Neglect*, **11**, 497–506.

Blanchard, G. (1987) Male victims of child sexual abuse: A portent of things to come. *Journal of Independent Social Work*, **1**(1), 19–27.

Bremmer, R. (1971) *Children and Youth in America* (Vol. 2). Cambridge, MA: Harvard University Press.

Brière, J. and Runtz, M. (1988) Symptomatology associated with childhood sexual victimization in a nonclinical adult sample. *Child Abuse and Neglect*, **12**, 51–9.

Budin, L. E. and Johnson, C. F. (1989) Sex abuse prevention programs: Offenders' attitudes about their efficacy. *Child Abuse and Neglect*, **13**(1), 77–87.

Butler, S. (1986) Thinking about prevention: A critical look. In M. Nelson and K. Clark (eds), *The Educator's Guide to Preventing Child Sexual Abuse*. Santa Cruz: Network Publications.

Caffey, J. (1946) Multiple fractures in the long bones of infants suffering from chronic subdural hematoma. *American Journal of Roentgenology*, **56**, 163–73.

Caffey, J. (1957) Some traumatic lesions in growing bones other than fractures and dislocations: Clinical and radiological features. *British Journal of Radiology*, **30**, 225–38.

Cantwell, H. B. (1981) Sexual abuse of children in Denver 1979: Reviewed with implications for pediatric intervention and possible prevention. *Child Abuse and Neglect*, **5**, 75–85.

Caplan, G. (1964) *Principles of Preventive Psychiatry*. New York: Basic Books.

*****Cohn, A. H. and Daro, D.** (1987) Is treatment too late? What ten years of evaluative research tell us. *Child Abuse and Neglect*, **9**(3), 319–28.

Conte, J. R. (1984) Progress in treating the sexual abuse of children. *Social Work*, **29**(3), 258–63.

Conte, J. R., Rosen, C., Saperstein, L. and Shermack, R. (1985) An evaluation of a program to prevent the sexual victimization of young children. *Child Abuse and Neglect*, **9**(3), 319–28.

Cotterill, A. M. (1988) The geographic distribution of child abuse in an inner city borough. *Child Abuse and Neglect*, **12**(4), 461–7.

Craine, L. S., Henson, C. E., Colliver, J. A. and MacLean, D. G. (1988) Prevalence of a history of sexual abuse among female psychiatric patients in a state hospital system. *Hospital and Community Psychiatry*, **39**(3), 300–4.

Creighton, S. J. (1985) An epidemiological study of abused children and their families in the United Kingdom between 1977 and 1982. *Child Abuse and Neglect*, **9**(4), 441–8.

Cupoli, J. M. and Sewell, P. M. (1988) One thousand and fifty-nine children with a chief complaint of sexual abuse. *Child Abuse and Neglect*, **12**, 151–62.

De Jong, A. R., Hervada, A. R. and Emmett, G. A. (1983) Epidemiologic variations in child sexual abuse. *Child Abuse and Neglect*, **7**, 155–62.

De Jong, A. R. and Rose, M. (1989) Frequency and significance of physical evidence in legally proven cases of child sexual abuse. *Pediatrics*, **84**(6), 1022–6.

Department of Health and Social Security (1988) *Report of the Inquiry into Child Abuse in Cleveland 1987*. London: HMSO.

Driver, E. (1989) Introduction. In E. Driver and A. Droisen (eds), *Child Sexual Abuse: Feminist Perspectives*. London: Macmillan.

Elliott, M. (1985) *Preventing Child Sexual Assault*. London: Bedford Square Press.

Emans, S. J., Woods, E. R., Flagg, N. T. and Freeman, A. (1987) Genital findings in sexually abused, symptomatic and asymptomatic girls. *Pediatrics*, **79**, 778–85.

Erickson, W. D., Walbek, N. H. and Seely, R. K. (1988) Behavior patterns of child molesters. *Archives of Sexual Behavior*, **17**(1), 77–86.

Faller, K. C. (1988) Criteria for judging the credibility of children's statements about their sexual abuse. *Child Welfare*, **67**(5), 389–401.

Farber, E. D., Showers, J., Johnson, C. F., Joseph, J. A. and Oshins, L. (1984) The sexual abuse of children: A comparison of male and female victims. *Journal of Clinical Child Psychology*, **13**, 294–7.

Finkel, M. A. (1989) Child sexual abuse: A physician's introduction to historical and medical validation. *Journal of the American Osteopathic Association*, **89**(9), 1143–9.

*Finkelhor, D. (1979) *Sexually Victimized Children*. New York: Free Press.

Finkelhor, D. (1980) Risk factors in the sexual victimization of children. *Child Abuse and Neglect*, **4**, 265–73.

Finkelhor, D. (1984) *Child Sexual Abuse: New Theory and Research*. New York: Free Press.

Finkelhor, D. (1986) Prevention: A review of programs and research. In D. Finkelhor (ed.), *A Sourcebook on Child Sexual Abuse*. Beverly Hills, CA: Sage Publications.

Finkelhor, D. and Browne, A. (1986) Initial and long-term effects: A conceptual framework. In D. Finkelhor (ed.), *A Sourcebook on Child Sexual Abuse*. Beverly Hills, CA: Sage Publications.

Finkelhor, D. and Hotaling, G. T. (1984) Sexual abuse in the National Incidence Study of Child Abuse and Neglect: An appraisal. *Child Abuse and Neglect*, **8**, 23–33.

Finkelhor, D., Hotaling, G., Lewis, I. A. and Smith, C. (1990) Sexual abuse in a national survey of adult men and women: Prevalence, characteristics, and risk factors. *Child Abuse and Neglect*, **14**(1), 19–28.

Fraser, B. G. (1981) Sexual child abuse: The legislation and the law in the United States. In P. B. Mrazek and C. H. Kempe (eds), *Sexually Abused Children and Their Families*. New York: Pergamon.

Fritz, G. S., Stoll, K. and Wagner, N. (1981) A comparison of males and females who were sexually molested as children. *Journal of Sex and Marital Therapy*, **7**(1), 54–9.

Fromuth, M. E. and Burkhart, B. R. (1987) Childhood sexual victimization among college men: Definitional and methodological issues. *Violence and Victims*, **2**(4), 241–53.

Fryer, G. E., Kraizer, S. K. and Miyoshi, T. (1987a) Measuring actual reduction of risk to child abuse: A new approach. *Child Abuse and Neglect*, **11**, 173–9.

Fryer, G. E., Kraizer, S. K. and Miyoshi, T. (1987b) Measuring children's retention of skills to resist stranger abduction: Use of the simulation technique. *Child Abuse and Neglect*, **11**, 181–5.

Gagnon, J. H. (1965) Female child victims of sex offenses. *Social Problems*, **13**(2), 176–92.

Garbarino, J. (1977) The human ecology of maltreatment: A conceptual model for research. *Journal of Marriage and the Family*, **39**, 721–36.

Garbarino, J. (1987) Children's response to a sexual abuse prevention program. A study of the Spiderman comic. *Child Abuse and Neglect*, **11**, 143–8.

Geddis, D. C. (1989) The diagnosis of sexual abuse of children. *New Zealand Medical Journal*, **102**(863), 99–100.

Gelardo, M. S. and Sanford, E. S. (1987) Child abuse and neglect: A review of the literature. *School Psychology Review*, **16**(2), 137–55.

Gelles, R. J. (1989) Child abuse and violence in single-parent families: Parent absence and economic deprivation. *American Journal of Orthopsychiatry*, **59**(4), 492–501.

Gil, D. (1970) *Violence Against Children: Physical Abuse in the United States*. Cambridge, MA: Harvard University Press.

Gillham, B. (1988) *Play Safe*. London: Methuen Children's Books.

Gillham, B. (1989) *Stay Safe*. Glasgow: BBC Educational Television.

Goldman, R. J. and Goldman, J. D. G. (1984) Perception of sexual experience in childhood: Relating normal experience to incest. *Australian Journal of Sex, Marriage and Family*, **5**(3), 159–66.

Goldman, R. J. and Goldman, J. D. G. (1988) The prevalence and nature of sexual abuse in Australia. *Australian Journal of Sex, Marriage and Family*, **9**(2), 94–106.

Goodwin, J., McCarty, T. and DiVasto, P. (1982) Physical and sexual abuse of the children of adult incest victims. In J. Goodwin (ed.), *Sexual Abuse: Incest Victims and Their Families*. Boston: John Wright.

Goodwin, J., Sahd, D. and Rada, R. T. (1979) Incest hoax: False accusations, false denials. *Bulletin of the American Academy of Psychiatry and the Law*, **6**, 269–76.

Groth, A. N., Burgess, A.W., Birnbaum, H. J. and Gary, T. S. (1978) A study of the child molester: Myths and realities. *Journal of the American Criminal Justice Association*, **41**, 17–22.

Hazzard, A. P., Webb, C. and Kleemeicr, C. (1988) Child sexual assault prevention programs: Helpful or unhelpful? Unpublished paper, Atlanta, GA: Emory University School of Medicine.

Herbert, C. P. (1987) Expert medical assessment in determining probability of alleged child sexual abuse. *Child Abuse and Neglect*, **11**, 213–21.

Hobbs, C. J. and Wynne, J. M. (1986) Buggery in childhood – a common syndrome of child abuse. *Lancet*, **2**, 792–6.

Hobbs, C. J. and Wynne, J. M. (1990) The sexually abused battered child. *Archives of the Diseases of Childhood*, **65**(4), 423–7.

Home Office (1983) *The British Crime Survey*. London: HMSO.

Home Office (1989) *Criminal Statistics England and Wales 1988*. London: HMSO.

Howitt, D. (1990) Expert opinion: Risky sexual abuse diagnosis. *Psychologist*, **3**(1), 15–17.

Indest, G. F. (1989) Medico-legal issues in detecting and proving the sexual abuse of children. *Journal of Sex and Marital Therapy*, **15**(2), 141–60.

Jaffe, A. C., Dynneson, L. and ten Bensel, R. W. (1975) Sexual abuse of children: An epidemiologic study. *American Journal of Diseases of Children*, **129**, 689–92.

James, J. and Meyerdring, J. (1977) Early sexual experiences as a factor in prostitution. *Archives of Sexual Behavior*, **7**(1), 31–42.

James, J., Womack, W. M. and Strauss, F. (1978) Physician reporting of sexual abuse of children. *Journal of the American Medical Association*, **240**(11), 1145–6.

Jason, J., Williams, S. L., Burton, A. and Rochat, R. (1982) Epidemiologic differences between sexual and physical child abuse. *Journal of the American Medical Association*, **247**(24), 3344–8.

Jones, D. P. H. and McQuiston, M. G. (1988) *Interviewing the Sexually Abused Child*. London: Gaskell.

Kempe, C. H., Silverman, F. N., Steele, B. B., Droegemueller, W. and Silver, H. K. (1962) The battered child syndrome. *Journal of the American Medical Association*, **181**, 17–24.

Kent, C. A. (1979) *Child Sexual Abuse Project: An Educational Program for Children*. Minneapolis: Hennepin County Attorney's Office Sexual Assault Services.

Kercher, G. A. and McShane, M. (1984) The prevalence of child sexual abuse victimization in an adult sample of Texas residents. *Child Abuse and Neglect*, **8**, 495–501.

Kinsey, A. C., Pomeroy, W. B. and Martin, C. E. (1948) *Sexual Behavior in the Human Male*. Philadelphia: W. B. Saunders.

Kinsey, A. C., Pomeroy, W. B. and Martin, C. E. (1953) *Sexual Behavior in the Human Female*. Philadelphia: W. B. Saunders.

Klingman, A., Melamed, B. G., Cuthbert, M. I. and Hermecz, D. A. (1984) Effects of participant modelling on information acquisition and skill utilization. *Journal of Consulting and Clinical Psychology*, **52**, 414–22.

Landis, J. (1956) Experiences of 500 children with adult sexual deviation. *Psychiatric Quarterly Supplement*, **30**, 91–109.

Leventhal, J. M. (1987) Programs to prevent sexual abuse: What outcomes should be measured? *Child Abuse and Neglect*, **11**, 169–72.

Levitt, E. E. (1957) The results of psychotherapy with children: An evaluation. *Journal of Consulting Psychology*, **21**, 189–96.

Levitt, E. E. (1971) Research on psychotherapy with children. In A. E. Bergin and S. L. Garfield (eds), *Handbook of Psychotherapy and Behavior Change*. New York: John Wiley.

MacMurray, B. K. (1989) The nonprosecution of sexual abuse and informal justice. *Journal of Interpersonal Violence*, **3**(2), 197–202.

Masson, J. M. (1984) *The Assault on Truth: Freud's Suppression of the Seduction Theory*. New York: Farrar, Straus and Giroux.

Miller-Perrin, C. L. and Wurtele, S. K. (1988) The child sexual abuse prevention movement: A critical analysis of primary and secondary approaches. *Clinical Psychology Review*, **8**(3), 313–29.

Mrazek, P., Lynch, M. and Bentovim, A. (1983) Sexual abuse of children in the United Kingdom. *Child Abuse and Neglect*, **7**, 147–53.

*Nash, C. L. and West, D. J. (1985) Sexual molestation of young girls: A retrospective survey. In D. J. West (ed.), *Sexual Victimisation*. Aldershot: Gower Publishing.

Nibert, D., Cooper, S. and Ford, J. (1989) Parents' observations of the effects of a sexual-abuse prevention program on preschool children. *Child Welfare*, **68**(5), 539–46.

Pinchbeck, I. and Hewitt, M. (1973) *Children in English Society* (Vol. 2). London: Routledge and Kegan Paul.

Rada, R. (1976) Alcoholism and the child molester. *Annals of the New York Academy of Science*, **273**, 492–6.

Reinhart, M. A. (1987) Sexually abused boys. *Child Abuse and Neglect*, **11**, 229–35.

*Repucci, N. D. and Haugaard, J. J. (1989) Prevention of child sexual abuse: Myth or reality? *American Psychologist*, **44**(10), 1266–75.

Rimsza, M. E. and Niggemann, E. H. (1982) Medical evaluation of sexually abused children: A review of 311 cases. *Pediatrics*, **69**(1), 8–14.

Risin, L. I. and McNamara, J. R. (1989) Validation of child sexual abuse: The psychologist's role. *Journal of Clinical Psychology*, **45**(1), 175–84.

Roberts, M. C., Alexander, K. and Fanurik, D. (1990) Evaluation of commercially available materials to prevent child abuse and abduction. *American Psychologist*, **45**(6), 782–3.

Rosenfeld, A. A. (1979) Incidence of a history of incest among 18 female psychiatric patients. *American Journal of Psychiatry*, **136**(6), 791–5.

Russell, A. B. and Trainor, C. M. (1984) *Trends in Child Abuse and Neglect*. Denver: American Humane Association.

*Russell, D. E. H. (1983) The incidence and prevalence of intrafamilial and extrafamilial sexual abuse of female children. *Child Abuse and Neglect*, **7**, 133–46.

Russell, D. E. H. (1984) The prevalence and seriousness of incestuous abuse: Stepfathers vs. biological fathers. *Child Abuse and Neglect*, **8**, 15–22.

Sackett, D. L., Haynes, R. B., Gibson, E. S., Hackett, B. C., Taylor, D. W., Roberts, R. S. and Johnson, A. L. (1975) Randomised clinical trial of strategies for improving medication compliance in primary hypertension. *Lancet*, **1**, 1205–7.

Sanford, L. T. (1980) *The Silent Children: A Parent's Guide to the Prevention of Child Sexual Abuse.* New York: Doubleday.

Sheldon, H. (1988) Childhood sexual abuse in adult female psychotherapy referrals: Incidence and implications for treatment. *British Journal of Psychiatry,* **152,** 107–11.

Showers, J., Farber, E. D., Joseph, J. A., Oshins, L. and Johnson, C. F. (1983) The sexual victimization of boys: A three-year survey. *Health Values: Achieving High Level Wellness,* **7,** 15–18.

Silverman, F. N. (1953) The Roentgen manifestations of unrecognised skeletal trauma in infants. *American Journal of Roentgenology,* **69**(3), 413–26.

*Sink, F. (1988) A hierarchical model for evaluation of child sexual abuse. *American Journal of Orthopsychiatry,* **58**(1), 129–35.

Sloan, J. (1989) Child abuse in schools. *Educational and Child Psychology,* **6**(1), 11–14.

*Soothill, K. L. and Gibbens, T. C. N. (1978) Recidivism of sexual offenders: A reappraisal. *British Journal of Criminology,* **18,** 267–76.

Soothill, K. L., Jack, A. and Gibbens, T. C. N. (1976) Rape: A 22 year cohort study. *Medical Science and Law,* **16,** 62–9.

Spencer, M. J. and Dunklee, P. (1986) Sexual abuse of boys. *Pediatrics,* **78**(1), 133–8.

*Steiner, H. and Taylor, M. (1988) Description and recording of physical signs in suspected child sexual abuse. *British Journal of Hospital Medicine,* **40**(5), 346–51.

Straus, M. A. and Gelles, R. J. (1986) Societal change and change in family violence from 1975 to 1985 as revealed by two national surveys. *Journal of Marriage and the Family,* **48,** 465–79.

Swan, H. L., Press, A. N. and Briggs, S. L. (1985) Child sexual abuse prevention: Does it work? *Child Welfare,* **64**(4), 395–405.

Swift, C. (1979) The prevention of sexual child abuse: Focus on the perpetrator. *Journal of Clinical Child Psychology,* **8**(2), 133–6.

Tharinger, D. J., Krivaska, J. J., Laye-McDonough, M., Jamison, L., Vincent, G. G. and Hedlund, A. D. (1988) Prevention of child sexual abuse: An analysis of issues, educational programs, and research findings. *School Psychology Review*, **17**(4), 614–34.

Tilelli, J. A., Turek, D. and Jaffe, A. (1980) Sexual abuse of children: Clinical findings and implications for management. *New England Journal of Medicine*, **302**, 319–23.

U.S. Department of Health and Human Services (1981) *Study Findings: National Study of the Incidence and Severity of Child Abuse and Neglect*. Washington, DC: U.S. Government Printing Office.

Vernon, A. and Hay, J. (1988) A preventative approach to child sexual abuse. *Elementary School Guidance and Counselling*, **22**(4), 306–12.

Vinnika, S. (1989) Child sexual abuse and the law. In E. Driver and A. Druisen (eds), *Child Sexual Abuse: Feminist Perspectives*. London: Macmillan.

Wild, N. J. (1986) Sexual abuse of children in Leeds. *British Medical Journal*, **292**, 1113–16.

Wolfe, D. A., MacPherson, T., Blount, R. and Wolfe, V. V. (1986) Evaluation of brief interventions for educating school children in awareness of physical and sexual abuse. *Child Abuse and Neglect*, **10**, 85–92.

Wooley, P. and Evans, W. (1955) Significance of skeletal lesions in infants resembling those of traumatic origin. *Journal of the American Medical Association*, **158**, 539–43.

Wurtele, S. K. (1987) School-based sexual abuse prevention programs: A review. *Child Abuse and Neglect*, **11**, 483–95.

Wurtele, S. K., Mars, S. R. and Miller-Perrin, C. L. (1987) Practice makes perfect? The role of participant modelling in sexual abuse prevention programs. *Journal of Consulting and Clinical Psychology*, **55**(4), 599–602.

Wurtele, S. K., Saslawsky, D. A., Miller-Perrin, C. L., Marrs, S. R. and Britcher, J. C. (1986) Teaching personal safety skills for potential prevention of sexual abuse: A comparison of treatments. *Journal of Consulting and Clinical Psychology*, **54**, 688–92.

Wyatt, G. E. (1985) The sexual abuse of Afro-American and White American women in childhood. *Child Abuse and Neglect*, **9**, 507–19.

Zax, M. and Cowen, E. L. (1976) *Abnormal Psychology: Changing Conceptions* (2nd edition). New York: Holt, Rinehart and Winston.

INDEX